LLANDUDNO

Queen of Welsh Resorts

Ivor Wynne Jones

Landmark Publishing

Published by
Landmark Publishing

The Oaks, Moor Farm Road West, Ashbourne, DE6 1HD
Tel: (01335) 347349 Fax: (01335) 347303
Email: landmark@clara.net Web: www.landmarkpublishing.co.uk

3rd edition

ISBN: 978 1 84306 429 9

Printed by TJ International, Cornwall

Design & reproduction by James Allsopp

Cover captions:

Front cover: The entrance to the Llandudno pier after the construction of The Pavilion.

Back cover Top: Performing birds entertain the crowds near to the entrance to the pier.

Page 1: Girls in Alice costume at the Lewis Carroll Memorial on the West Shore in 1988.

CONTENTS

AUTHOR'S FOREWORD TO 2ND EDITION

Long since out of print, my original *Llandudno, Queen of the Welsh Resorts,* has been the town's handbook for more than a quarter of a century. During that time the resort has seen many changes that are now embodied in this totally new book. Having compiled all Llandudno Urban Council's annual tourist guides from their inception in 1968, I wrote the first edition of *Llandudno, Queen of the Welsh Resorts* in response to a Caernarvonshire County Planning Committee plea for an adequate guidebook to Llandudno, when they realised there was no reference work to help draft their Great Orme Conservation Survey in 1973.

This 2002 replacement volume is more than twice the length of the original and contains a different set of illustrations, but it retains the original friendly format based on a series of topographical walks. These journeys through time may be followed on foot or in an arm chair, observing the town's historical kaleidoscope as one proceeds.

A topographical progression fragments the chronology, because it nips back and forth in time, but it enables the reader to avoid plodding through page after page of the distant past in order to reach the familiar aspects of what really is the unchallengeable Queen of Wales's holiday resorts. Unlike a more conventional chronological history, *Llandudno, Queen of Welsh Resorts* is able to incorporate first-hand anecdotal gems from half a century of journalistic involvement with everything of any importance in the life of the town. As the *Daily Post's* last Chief Welsh Correspondent I was able to attend anything affecting Llandudno, both in the town and well beyond, in such august corridors as the House of Commons, Welsh Office, Westminster Abbey, Oxford University, or anywhere in the world where Llandudno citizens made news, such as Rome, Cairo, Paris, Troyes, Berlin, Mametz, Wormhout, New York, Orlando, Washington, etc. Snippets of Llandudno history harvested during such journalistic excursions are now given some written permanence.

Ivor Wynne Jones, Llandudno, June 2002

WILL BE SOLD BY PUBLIC AUCTION,

At the Castle Hotel, Conway,

ON TUESDAY, THE 28th, AND WEDNESDAY, THE 29th AUGUST, 1849,

AT ONE O'CLOCK PRECISELY,

BY MR. LLOYD,

ELIGIBLE BUILDING LAND,

IN THAT

ROMANTIC, PICTURESQUE, AND INTERESTING

WATERING PLACE, LLANDUDNO,

AT THE FOOT OF

THE GREAT ORME'S HEAD,

AND IN FRONT OF

LLANDUDNO AND CONWAY BAYS.

THE TENURE IS LEASEHOLD FOR 75 YEARS,

RENEWABLE MUCH ON THE SAME TERMS AS THOSE IN PRACTICE BY THE CORPORATION OF LIVERPOOL.

A COPY OF THE

BUILDING REGULATIONS,

AND THE

TABLE SHOWING THE SCALE ON WHICH LEASES WILL BE RENEWED,

WITH A

LITHOGRAPHIC MAP OF THE GLODDAETH ESTATE,

BELONGING TO THE HON. E. M. LLOYD MOSTYN, M.P.,

AND THE ADJACENT COUNTRY,

MAY BE HAD OF

Messrs. WILLIAMS and M'LEOD, Solicitors, 3, Paper-buildings, London ;
Messrs. CUDDON, Norwich, and 8, Gray's Inn-square, London ;
Mr. LLOYD, Auctioneer, Park-place, Ruthin ;
Mr. JOHN WILLIAMS, Bodafon, Llandudno, near Conway ; and of
Messrs. WILLIAMS and JONES, 28, St. James's-road, Liverpool ;

TO WHOM ALL REFERENCES AND APPLICATIONS MUST BE MADE.

July. 1849.

The 1849 announcement for the auction that created modern Llandudno.

THE FIRST BATHERS

LLANDUDNO was an isolated mountain hamlet of mystery and intrigue when Dr. Robert Wittie launched his novel sea-bathing cult in 1667. Virtually cut off from the mainland, by the marshes on which the Victorian town was to be built, 17th century Llandudno was a community of seamen-farmers, living in primitive cottages on the eastern slopes of the Great Orme headland, amid the remains of prehistoric tombs and disused copper mines. They were served by the ancient parish church of St. Tudno, although they had to cross the mountain to get to it and had never seen their rector, the sinecure living having been vested in the Archdeaconry of Merioneth since 1504. Nearer to hand was their ale-house (on the site of Llwynonn Terrace), licensed shortly after the passing of the 1603 Act requiring inn-keepers and ale-house keepers to provide one or more beds for the lodging of strangers. The mountain hollows were fertile, and nearly a thousand acres of common land, both on the Orme and on the marshes – called Morfa Isa – offered good rough grazing. The surrounding sea provided good catches of fish and an abundance of shipwrecks and plunder.

On the other side of the marsh there were four sinister mansions: Penrhyn, Gloddaeth, Bodysgallen and the new Marl, the homes of families deeply embroiled in the political and religious machinations of the period. Penrhyn had long been the scene of Jesuit conspiracy, under the protection of the Pugh family. It was in a cave on the Little Orme, forming part of the Penrhyn property, that Robert Pugh assisted a group of priests to print *Y Drych Cristionogawl* ("The Christian Mirror") in 1585. Another Robert Pugh of Penrhyn was accused of being involved in the Titus Oates plot, and was imprisoned at Newgate where he died, aged 70, in 1679. A few decades later the last heir of the Pughs was mysteriously murdered, his body remaining hidden until the beginning of the 19th century.

Gloddaeth was the scene of the arrest of another priest, Father John Bennet, in 1582. He was sentenced to death but, after a long period of imprisonment at Ludlow Castle, was deported, to live on until 1625. The Mostyn family of Gloddaeth was skilled in riding political controversy and they lived through this incident with ever-ascending power, eventually to engineer the enclosure of the Llandudno Common in 1843 and establish their leasehold grip on the present town.

Closely associated with Gloddaeth, was the nearby Bodysgallen, a name mentioned as early as 1350 when it appears to have been part of Gloddaeth estate. An ancient tower forms the core of the present house, which dates from 1620, with additions in 1700, 1884, 1894, 1905 and 1914. It was owned by Richard Mostyn in the 16th century but passed by marriage to the Wynn family, who built the 1620 section. It returned to the Mostyns, again by marriage, in 1776.

Marl was bought in 1627 by John Williams. As Archbishop of York he garrisoned Conwy Castle for King Charles in the Civil War of 1642, but a royalist army had to storm the castle to turn him out in 1645 and soon after that Archbishop Williams joined Cromwell, thus saving his skin by being on the winning side when the war ended. He died at Gloddaeth in 1650. Marl was rebuilt in 1661 and the Williams family, whose principal home was at Craig-y-don, near Beaumaris, eventually obtained a share of the Llandudno Common, under the 1843 land snatch, although they soon disposed of it in the freehold lots which make up most of the present Craig-y-don area of the town and Penrhyn Bay.

Gogarth, the manor house on the southwestern slopes of the Great Orme, was nothing more than a ruin (now mistakenly called an abbey). It was built in about 1300 as the palace of the Bishops of Bangor, a gift from King Edward I for Bishop Anian's christening of the first English Prince of Wales at Caernarfon.

An 1852 watercolour of embryo Llandudno, by R.Green, a pupil of David Cox. It shows, from left to right, Pwll-y-gwichiaid, Tŷ John Jeffreys, Osborne House under construction (the artist's having imagined what it might look like), Morannedd, Sea View and Craig-y-don, with Tŷ Gwyn in the foreground. Below is a drawing from Pwll-y-gwichiaid in about 1842, showing the old Welsh Baptist chapel in the centre, and the original road to the beach.

Beyond stretched the great unknown, a land of mystery and violence, of disease and strange battles in a war that the people of Llandudno did not understand. Roads into the unknown were little more than meandering tracks of mud. Once a year the parishioners would be conscripted for six days of unpaid labour, depositing stone on the highway, but there is no reason to suppose the ruling landowners were any different from those in the rest of the country – and the stone would be placed where it would best serve the mansions. The sea offered an alternative passage into the world but it was equally sinister. Arabs, seeking white slaves for sale in North Africa, dominated the Irish Sea until 1642. Opposing fleets of the English Civil War cleared out the Arabs but their pressgangs captured even greater numbers of Welsh slaves to man their ships.

Thus all strangers arriving at Llandudno would be regarded with suspicion. Their slow progress across the marsh, by the two most practical routes, close to either shore, would be observed from the mountain hamlet. In the eyes of the residents there could be no good reason for a visit from the outer world. All strangers were snoopers of one kind or another for this was the great age of spies and informers, of plots and counter plots, and of outlawed Jesuits, recusants, Royalists, regicides, Jacobites and many more.

It was against this background that Llandudno became a centre of espionage during William III's campaign against the Irish rebellion under the deposed James. In 1690, on the eve of the Battle of the Boyne in which he was to lose his life while leading a cavalry charge, Frederick Hermann, Marshal the Count of Schomberg – second-in-command of the army with which William of Orange landed in England in 1688 – reported to the king that a man named Thomson, living on the Great Orme, was in regular communication with the Irish insurgents. Who was Thomson, a strange name for the Welsh speaking community at Llandudno? Was he a descendant of James the Scot, named in 1616 as licensee of the Llandudno ale-house? The Earl of Shrewsbury reported that those in correspondence with the enemy used Thomson's house, and that "his son, who commands an armed ketch, goes every week to collect the letters."

The 17th century was the period of transition, from the primitive existence that had not changed very much since the Middle Ages to the civilisation that came with the discoveries of the ensuing 200 years. Llandudno knew nothing – and certainly would not have cared if it had known – about the controversy which was raging at Scarborough over the properties of the latter town's spa water, and which culminated in 1667 with the publication of Dr. Robert Wittie's *Scarborough Spaw* in which he extolled the village's unique virtue of possessing both a spa and the sea, a combination guaranteed to cure "hypochondriack melancholy and windiness... scurvy, asthmatic complaints, habitual costiveness and sexual indispositions." Britain's first seaside resort was born.

By 1702 the cult was sufficiently established for Sir John Floyer, in conjunction with Edward Baynard, to publish a *History of Cold Bathing* in which he advocated sea-bathing as a cure for just about everything, including cancer, rheumatism, ulcers, deafness, asthma, hernia, corns, leprosy, consumption, venereal diseases, tumours, a disordered mind, and, perhaps most significantly of all:

> Cold bathing has this good alone;
> It makes old John to hug old Joan!
> And does fresh kindnesses entail
> On a wife tasteless, old and stale.

Floyer recommended the drinking of sea-water, this being an extension of the practice which had already begun at the older inland bathing spas such as Bath and Buxton. The cult was taken a stage further by Dr. Richard Russell who claimed to have obtained medical degrees at

Early steamship visitors had to be carried ashore. One of the town's early attractions was the Hydropathic & Winter Residence, still recognisable within the modern Hydro Hotel.

Padua, but whose qualifications were challenged by his London rivals. In 1752 he published his *Dissertation on the use of seawater,* which ran into four editions. With overtones of the primitive nature-cures of the previous century Dr. Russell proclaimed the sea to be a universal remedy, so long as it was used in conjunction with one of his patent concoctions, incorporating such things as crabs' eyes, viper flesh, snails and tincture of woodlice.

A pint of sea-water, taken each morning, would produce "three or four smart stools," said Dr. Russell. To complete his treatment patients had to take a dip in the sea. "A perfect repose of the body, and calmness of the mind, is to be observed before the use of the cold bath, and all exercise of the parts affected must be forborne, that the fibres by these means, when they contract themselves, may have the greater force to overcome any obstruction," he wrote.

This pseudo-scientific nonsense appealed to 18th century London where traditional medicine had little to offer against the terrible diseases of the day. To cater more effectively for his wealthy patrons Dr. Russell opened a clinic in 1754 at the fishing village of Brightelmstone, only a day's coach-ride from London. All that was required to make sea-bathing a national craze was the arrival at the clinic, in 1783 of the impetuous young Prince of Wales.

Today a marble tablet on a hotel wall marks the site of Dr. Russell's clinic. It says: "If you seek his monument look around," and one beholds the Brighton which grew out of Brightelmstone. If one looks far enough one sees Llandudno and all the other seaside resorts that stemmed from Dr. Russell's hydropathic clinic.

By 1859 Llandudno had its own *Medical Guide* for visitors, written by Dr. J.M. Coley, of Pendyffryn, who listed an impressive curriculum vitae. His past appointments included physician to His Serene Highness the Duke of Aremberg, to Prince de Vismes et de Ponthieu, to the British Legation in Brussels and to the Royal Pimlico Dispensary. He took up residence in the new Llandudno in 1858, and said invalids and convalescents would find "no locality uniting more charmingly a mild seaside residence with mountain scenery."

"Here the politician, the student, the merchant and the lawyer, like the Roman orators after their arduous exertions in the forum, can find repose, and repair the loss of health occasioned by mental or physical exhaustion; and the naturalist, the botanist, and the antiquarian can pursue their favourite studies, free from the corroding cares and distractions of civic and official life."

Unlike his Scarborough and Brighton predecessors who believed sea bathing to be a cure for everything, Dr. Coley advised Llandudno visitors to keep out of the sea if they suffered from apoplexy, epilepsy, hysteria, fainting fits, incipient pulmonary consumption, chronic bronchitis, dysentery, diarrhoea, spitting of blood, organic diseases within chest and abdomen, valvular disease in the heart, inflammation in the kidneys, enlargement of the liver, spleen, etc, or anyone who did not see a glow on the skin after sea bathing.

For everyone else 15 to 30 minutes in the sea would be beneficial, especially when the tide was rising, and if followed by a walk up the Great Orme to breathe "the light and unadulterated atmosphere and increased supply of oxygen to be found on the side of the mountain." Dr. Coley said the warm sea-bathing available at the Baths (on the site of the present Grand Hotel) was beneficial for countless ailments, something not generally appreciated in Britain.

And so Llandudno emerged as a sea-bathing health centre and if one looks beyond its shores one can find the Cape Town sea-bathing suburb of Llandudno, created in 1903 beside what became Llandudno Bay. It nestles between two headlands, though less impressively than the Welsh original. The South African imitation has a very popular neighbouring nudist beach, with shades of the early naturist philosophy that brought our resort into being.

An abandoned cottage on the Great Orme, in 1864. The picture below is the shop of William Prichard, "Grocer & Draper," founded in 1831 at the junction of Old Road and Church Walks.

An early engraving of embryo Llandudno.
By the time the photograph below was taken in 1875 modern North Parade was complete.

Completion in 1858 of the first section of St.George's Pier, with toll hut for collector Robert Jones (third from the left).

The completed pier is seen here in an 1859 photograph showing the flat John, used for carrying copper ore to Amlwch. The small boat in the foreground is the St.George, owned by David Hughes, Cambria.

Before the concept of Llandudno as a health resort there were plans for using the sand dunes to create a new town to be called St George, complete with a breakwater across the bay, to serve as a rail and ferry terminal for the London-Dublin traffic. The union of the parliaments of Great Britain and Ireland in 1801, to create the United Kingdom, resulted in the building of Thomas Telford's famous A5 Holyhead-London road to speed the journey of politicians and mail. With the subsequent advent of the steam railway there was an immediate search for a faster route.

A team of surveyors and entrepreneurs crossed the shallow dunes on the Creuddyn or Llandudno isthmus in the reign of William IV, and mapped out a breakwater between the Great and Little Orme headlands. They paid no attention to the village of Llandudno on the slopes of the Great Orme, and the old parish name did not feature in the November 1836 Bill presented to Parliament by the St.George's Harbour & Railway Company. The promoters calculated the distances as 230 miles (370 km) from London to what they called Ormes Bay, and 96 miles (154 km) from Ormes Bay to Kingstown (now known as Dun Laoghaire), and said the total journey time from London to Dublin would be 19½ hours.

When asked to report on the Ormes Bay scheme, the Admiralty Hydrographer said that whilst Holyhead was undoubtedly the best port, any plan for a railway would be frustrated by the impediment of the Menai Strait, so that an alternative terminal would be necessary. However, the Bill was defeated when debated during the 1837 Parliamentary session.

In 1837 the Irish Railway Commission said the London-Dublin journey time could be shortened by 1½ hours compared with the Ormes Bay scheme by constructing a railway from Worcester, via Bala, Ffestiniog, Tremadog and Pwllheli, to a proposed new harbour at Porthdinllaen, from where the distance to Kingstown was only 70 miles (113 km) The notion of converting Porthdinllaen shelter, in the notoriously hazardous Caernarfon Bay, into a harbour of refuge protected by a breakwater had been around since 1804, and the Porthdinllaen Harbour Company was formed in 1806, complete with grand office just above the shoreline. In 1808 a Bill was presented to Parliament for Porthdinllaen to supersede Holyhead as the port for the Irish mail traffic, at a cost of £12,000 – and it actually received Royal assent. This was the plan revived in 1837. The company and its headquarters (now two houses called Whitehall and Old Whitehall) still exist, owned by the National Trust, but there is no public road to this isolated community of 18 tenanted houses and a summer pub, whose trade comes from people walking along the beach from Nefyn in good weather.

Yet a third alternative to the Llandudno proposal was put forward by the Chester & Crewe Railway Company, who in 1838 commissioned George Stephenson to survey a line from Chester to Holyhead – and also to report on the Porthdinllaen plan. In September of that year the promoters of the Ormes Bay scheme convened a meeting at Chester to try to revive their own plan under the new name of the St.George's Harbour & Chester Railway. The meeting was told the cost of creating a breakwater and harbour between the Great Orme and the Little Orme would be £200,000, to which an Ormes Bay to Chester railway would cost £600,000. These figures, it was said, compared very favourably with Charles B. Vignoles' plan for a line across Mid Wales to a new harbour at Porthdinllaen, estimated to cost £3,500,000.

Wehnert and Ashdown's 1854 concept, showing the intended St. George's railway terminus in North Parade.

That prompted the *Railway Magazine* of October 1838 to declare Porthdinllaen to be an extremely difficult place to which to lay a railway. It also noted the business community's argument that if the Irish ferry passed Holyhead why should its passengers be put ashore at Ormes Bay instead of continuing to Liverpool? It was for these reasons that the directors of the Chester & Crewe Railway Company had held back on the Ormes Bay scheme, which they had been urged to take up, said the magazine.

However, all was not lost for the proposed town of St. George, in so-called Ormes Bay, for the magazine's writer added: "I am perfectly satisfied that the only rational plan is to lay down a railway from Chester to Holyhead via the Ormesheads. No half measures will stand long in these days."

There were then only eight residents of Llandudno entitled to vote in Parliamentary elections: George Badcock, tenant of Bodafon; Thomas Davies, occupier of Pentre Isa; John Evans, Bodhyfryd, freeholder of Tŷ'n-y-coed farm; Peter Jones, tenant of Pwllygwichiaid; Roger Lester, leaseholder of Bodnant; John Lester, leaseholder of Tŷ Coch; John Roberts, Tŷ Newydd, freeholder of Penyffrith; and David Williams, tenant of Tŷ Draw.

In November 1839 the Treasury appointed Lieut-Colonel Sir Frederick Smith and Professor Peter Barlow to serve as Commissioners to inquire into and report upon all three rival schemes. In April 1840 they reported their preference for a North Wales coastal route, saying there would be no engineering difficulties in the Ormes Bay scheme, which would require only one tunnel, near the western end of the line (i.e. Penmaenhead). However, the Commissioners had consulted the Admiralty, and in January 1840 Rear-Admiral Sir James Gordon and Captain Beechey had dismissed both Ormes Bay and Porthdinllaen as "mere roadsteads," leaving only the Holyhead option. With no other means of bridging the Menai Strait it was suggested that passengers could cross the 1826 suspension bridge in horse carriages, to railway stations at either end. George Stephenson told the Commissioners a railway carriage weighed five tons, the same as a coach and four horses. The carriages could be hauled across, one at a time, with a rope and fixed engines at either end, so as to prevent the oscillation that would occur if they were horse-drawn.

A House of Commons Select Committee was set up in June 1842 to look into the whole problem and it was at that stage the Ormes Bay proposals dropped out of the argument. Undaunted, promoters of the Ormes Bay route emerged in 1843 with the title of the North Wales & Dublin Railway & Harbour Company. They suggested that a railway from Chester to termi-

Luggage porter William Jones's hut in which Llandudno was planned in December 1846, during a rainstorm conference between Edward Lloyd Mostyn and Liverpool surveyor Owen Williams. Below is a modern photograph of St. Tudno's church, from which the town takes its name.

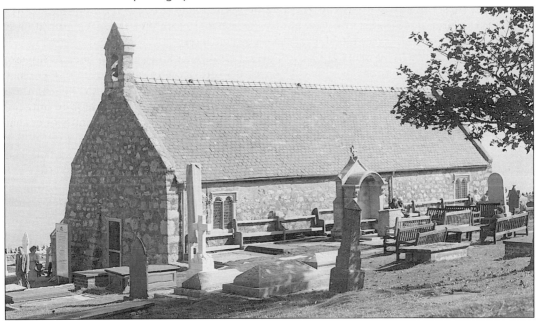

nate in either Ormes Bay – still no mention of Llandudno – or Conwy would save £2m or more on the costs of the Chester & Crewe Railway Company's scheme. The additional mileage to Holyhead would be a waste of public money and out of proportion to the time saved, they added.

The Chester & Holyhead Railway Company was incorporated by an Act of Parliament of 4 July 1844, with a requirement of £2m capital for the estimated cost of the line (it actually cost £3,084,000). Robert Stephenson, 41, was appointed engineer for the project, on the recommendation of his father George Stephenson, who had surveyed the route in 1838. The first sod was ceremonially cut at Conwy, on St. David's Day 1845. The line was opened from Chester to Bangor on 1 May 1848, and 200 guests attended a celebration dinner at Conwy on the 17th, presided over by the Hon. E.M. Lloyd Mostyn, MP. "Thirty years ago," he said, "a mail coach left Conwy at 12 o'clock on Wednesday and did not reach London until 6 o'clock on Friday morning. It cost seven guineas (£7.35) for an inside fare to London, independent of incidental expenses on the journey. Now in seven hours one can travel in a comfortable armchair, at the cost of a mere trifle." (The fares were 3d per mile for a 1st Class seat; 2$\frac{1}{2}$d [1p] 2nd Class; and 1$\frac{1}{2}$d for 3rd Class).

The line from Llanfairpwllgwyngyll to Holyhead was opened on 1 August 1848. Robert Stephenson's plan for crossing the Menai Strait in a pair of wrought-iron square tubs was the subject of a separate Act of Parliament (30 June 1845), and the Britannia Bridge was opened on 18 March 1850 to complete the railway from Holyhead harbour to London Euston. The London & North Western Railway took over the running of the Chester & Holyhead Railway in 1856, and absorbed the company in 1858.

Thus the resort we now know as Llandudno escaped being called St. George, but that was not the end of the story. The St. George's Harbour & Railway Company re-emerged, Phoenix-like, with an Act of Parliament of August 1853 authorising them to build a 3$\frac{1}{2}$ mile (5.6 km) branch line from a new Llandudno Junction station into the newly emerging town of Llandudno. The Act also envisaged a harbour with breakwater, lighthouses, piers, docks, locks, quays, wharfs, landing places and all the paraphernalia of a big port. The double track railway was opened in 1858 to main line standards. Llandudno became one of the most important railway stations in Britain, and by the 1930s would handle 81 train arrivals a day on a typical Bank Holiday Saturday.

With an echo of the 1836 abortive Ormes Bay project, the St. George's Harbour & Railway Company defiantly built a token pier in 1858, so as to preserve their Parliamentary rights, which were subject to a time limit. It was 242 ft (74m) long, 16$\frac{1}{2}$ ft (5m) wide, 30 ft (9m) above the beach, and stood on 16 wooden piles, north of the present Grand Hotel. Drawings produced at the time show the envisaged continuation of the railway across the present town to a cutting through North Parade, to link up with the pier – which was demolished by a storm in 1859.

St. George lived on in new Llandudno in such names as St. George's Church, St. George's Crescent, St. George's Place, St. George's Hall, St. George's School and St. George's Hotel. The original St. George was an Iraqi Arab who was beheaded in Palestine early in the 4th century, and buried at Lydda, which used to be called the City of St. George (and which Israel has renamed Lod). According to Arab tradition the beast he slew was not the Red Dragon of Wales but a Libyan monster. Goodness knows why Edward III appointed St. George patron saint of England, with his distinctive flag of a red cross on a white field. What a narrow escape for Llandudno! Even worse, while the various St. George's harbour plans were floating around there was a plan to make Llandudno an export point for the collieries of Denbighshire, in which event the town would have been given the name of Port Wrexham.

Demolition in 1909 of the 1840 semaphore station on the Great Orme summit.
Below, car No.5 of the Great Orme Railway leaves Victoria Station in Church Walks.

Petula Clark and the Llandudno bathing machines during the filming of The Card in 1951. The photograph below was taken about a decade before Arnold Bennett wrote The Card in 1911.

MORE STYLISH THAN SOME

3

"LLANDUDNO is more stylish than either Rhyl or Blackpool, and not dearer," wrote social chronicler Arnold Bennett, in his delightful novel *The Card,* published in 1911. He epitomised the Queen of the Western Watering Places (an accolade bestowed upon Llandudno by the *Liverpool Mercury* as long ago as 1864), for modern Llandudno still retains all that is best of the stylish resort designed to satisfy the leisure needs of Victorian society.

The origins of the resort are to be found in an Enclosure Award of 1848, when Parliamentary Commissioners apportioned the 955 acres (387 hectares) of parish common land among the principal freeholders. Nowadays the Award would be described as a confidence trick but in 1842, when the idea was canvassed among the smallholders on the Great Orme, no one dared argue with the Right Reverend Christopher Bethell who, as Lord Bishop of Bangor, was also Lord of the Manor of Gogarth and "front" name for the scheming landlords. (The Lordship of the Manor of Gogarth passed to the University of Wales in 1920, to be held in trust as part of the arrangement for disestablishing the Anglican Church in Wales and separating it from the Church of England. In 1988 the title was auctioned for £11,000 to Stanley Mitchell, of Elstree, Hertfordshire – a person completely unknown in Llandudno).

The 1842 Bishop of Bangor was rewarded with 18 acres (7 hectares), his absentee sinecure rector with five, and the poor perpetual curate got a quarter-acre with which to feed himself. In exchange for their grazing rights on the Common the powerless parishioners got 1½ acres (0.6 hectares) to be used as a recreation area and 30 square yards (25sqm) for a communal well. Most of the Common – 832 acres (337 hectares) of it – went to Edward Lloyd Mostyn who, as MP for Flintshire, had introduced the Eglwysrhos, Llandudno and Llangystennin Enclosure Bill to Parliament. Born in 1805, he was the son and heir to the first Baron Mostyn (a title created in 1831) whom he succeeded in 1854. He was also the nephew of the childless Lady Champneys who had inherited the Gloddaeth estate upon the death of her unmarried brother, Sir Thomas Mostyn (6th and last baronet), in 1831. The enclosure Award apportioned the Common in ratio to the area of one's free-holding.

Between the local Enclosure Act's becoming law in 1843, and the completion of the apportionment Award five years later, the land-grabbing exercise took a dramatic turn when Owen Williams, a 32-years-old Anglesey-born surveyor, chanced to visit the Great Orme a year after the death of Lady Champneys. He was in business in Liverpool and it was from there that he accompanied a friend who was attending a meeting of shareholders of one of the Great Orme copper mines.

"It was on a very bright summer day in 1846 that John Jones, a friend in Liverpool, happened to say he was going to a mine meeting at Llandudno, and invited me to accompany him, saying it would be a nice little run," reminisced Owen Williams half-a-century later, after he had retired to Plas Lodwig, Bangor.

They sailed from Liverpool in a ship trading with the Menai Strait, and were rowed ashore at Llandudno. They completed the journey by walking a plank affixed to two wheels, a device made to accommodate a trickle of early Victorian traders and adventurers visiting the mining village on the slopes of the Orme. The wheeled plank was operated by William Jones, Bodhyfryd, owner of a little hut above high water mark labelled: "A spring cart for hire – luggage to & from all parts of the town. Apply here." As they handed over their luggage, for conveyance to the King's Head Inn, Owen Williams turned to his friend and said: "What a charming watering-place this would make."

He was later to recall: "Then there was no town – only a few thatched cottages in which the miners resided. Near the cottages, fronting the sea, was a small farm known as Pwllygwichiaid."

While his friends inspected their investment in the Tŷ Gwyn mine (named after a farm near the present Pier gates), Owen Williams took his first look at the limestone mountain of mystery with a Viking name (*orm* = serpent). He found a remote self-sufficient community of a thousand people who earned their living from mining or farming, or from supplying the basic needs of each other. They had a new church, three nonconformist chapels and eight taverns which, with their thatched cottages, were concentrated on or around the steep hill we now call Old Road, with the beginnings of an overflow into Church Walks. There were also about twenty-five squatters' hovels, dotted about the Common on either side of what is now Mostyn Street.

Strolling up Old Road, Williams found the village soon gave way to a man-made desert of deep shafts amid mounds of light-brown rock spoil, with a lofty engine house (built in 1835) belching smoke and steam in the middle of it all. Beyond, on the 679 ft (207m). high summit of the Great Orme, there was a semaphore station, rebuilt in 1841 on the site of an 1827 installation, and forming part of a signalling chain from Holyhead to Liverpool. On the northern cliffs the old parish church of St. Tudno, from which Llandudno took its name, had been reduced to a roofless shell after a gale in 1839.

From his lofty vantage point Williams looked down on the narrow isthmus of low-lying marshland and sand dunes stretching to the Little Orme, two miles away. The view confirmed his initial impression that this was an ideal site for a fashionable new seaside resort, enjoying the advantage of two shores, back to back – an idea he discussed with the mine shareholders when he rejoined them for a meal at the King's Head. This conversation was dutifully relayed to Gloddaeth hall by John Williams, 35-years-old Caernarfon-born farmer of Bodafon farm (a 250 acre [101 hectare] holding on the opposite side of the marsh) who, as well as being secretary to the Tŷ Gwyn Mine Company, was also the Mostyn family's land agent.

"Two or three days later, I received a letter from the Hon. Edward Mostyn, who resided at Gloddaeth, inviting me to call upon him on business," reminisced Owen Williams, shortly before his death in 1902. Accustomed to instant obedience, the Mostyns had to make do with an exchange of letters in which Owen Williams said it would be several months before he could find the time to revisit Llandudno. And so the historic encounter was delayed until the spring of

Bath chairs, hauled by a "chairman," quietly vanished from the Promenade during World War One, when the summer sickness of the idle rich was placed in perspective.

Regal visitors
Top; Left: Prince Gorchakov, 1858.
Right: Emperor Napoleon III, 1874
Below; Left: Queen Elisabeth of
Roumania, 1890. Right: Princess
Margaret, 1951.

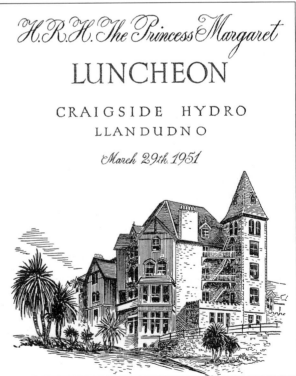

H.R.H. The Princess Margaret

LUNCHEON

CRAIGSIDE HYDRO
LLANDUDNO

March 29th, 1951

1847, when Owen Williams was again rowed ashore from a passing ship. He and Mostyn, then aged 42, took shelter from the rain in William Jones's hut on the beach and it was there that they planned the Llandudno we see today.

While Richard Yates, of Whittington, mapped out the Common, for the Enclosure Award he signed on 25 April 1848, Owen Williams surveyed the same land for an auction of leasehold building plots on 28 and 29 August 1849. "An hotel is much wanted and any person who is prepared to purchase land and to erect one will be very liberally dealt with," wrote Williams in his auction brochure. His town map included plans for a 35-bedroom establishment to be known as the Mostyn Arms (the nucleus of the present Royal Hotel, in Church Walks).

Llandudno, he wrote, was within 2½ hours sailing time of Liverpool. "The stranger will be surprised to find himself transported in so short a time into a country where the language spoken is as Greek to him, and where he will not be understood by many of the natives without the aid of an interpreter," added Williams, by way of a reminder that Welsh was the natural language of the area.

"The lowest classes bear indications of great poverty, yet they seem to enjoy good health," he continued. "Their cottages are built of stone and, in general, are kept very clean. Most of them are so dark that on first entering they have a very gloomy appearance. The women are of middle size, though more frequently below than above it. Their features are often very pretty but in point of figure they are in general uninteresting. Few hats are worn by the females in this district, but the natives have their characteristics and some of them afford much amusement to the visitors."

Not surprisingly, the auction (which took place at Plas Mawr, Conwy, and not at the Castle Hotel, as advertised) was something of a flop, despite a big attendance. Seven plots were sold on the first day, and 37 on the second, with another four sold by private treaty on the following day. Prices ranged from 1s to 1s 6d (5p to 7½p) a square yard (0.3sqm).

Only twenty-four property occupiers in the parish of Llandudno were entitled to vote at Parliamentary elections, in the register of 16 August 1848. They were: George Brookes, Victoria; John Hughes, Old Mine; John Jones, of Price Street, Liverpool, Tŷ Gwyn Mine; John Jones, Llwynonn; Owen Jones, Plas Uchaf; Thomas Jones, Frondeg; William Jones, Tŷ Newydd; David Jones, Tŷ Draw; John Lester, Tŷ Coch; Roger Lester, Bodnant; Owen Owens, Pendyffryn; William Owens, King's Head; Hugh Parry, Tan-y-frondeg; Robert Parry, Tŷ'n-y-maes; William Parry, Tŷ Gwyrdd; Thomas Parry, Fron; William Prichard, "own occupation"; John Roberts, Tŷ-newydd, freeholder of Penyffrith; Meredith Vickers, of Whitford Street, Holywell, Tŷ Gwyn Mine; William Williamson, of Greenfield, Holywell, Tŷ Gwyn Mine; Henry Williams, Cwlach; John Williams, Pen-y-fron; Robert Williams, George & Dragon; and Robert Williams, freeholder of Pant.

By 1851 the population of Llandudno had crept up to 1,131, of whom 743 were natives of the parish. The biggest immigrant element was the 40 born at Amlwch, in Anglesey, where they had acquired skills in the copper mining industry. Nearly 200 of Llandudno's inhabitants were listed as miners in the 1851 census. Local government came to Llandudno in July 1854 with the election of the first Board of Improvement Commissioners, backed by a local Act of Parliament giving them wide powers. They chose Thomas Mostyn to be their chairman. He was the 24-years-old son of Edward Mostyn and in May had succeeded his father as MP for Flintshire. The first clerk to the Commissioners was John Williams, of Bodafon farm, faithful agent of the Mostyns. A plaque in St.George's church records that John Williams (who was buried at Llanrhos in June 1876) was churchwarden at Llandudno for 37 years, chairman of the Conwy Board of Guardians for 27 years, and influenced the building of the St. George's and Holy Trinity churches and the National School.

Llandudno's first omnibus ran between St.George's Hotel and Conwy railway station, before the opening of Llandudno station. Here it is seen outside the hotel in 1905. The 60 h.p. Mercedes, below, driven by Gerald Higginbottom, was the first car to ascend the Great Orme, in September 1903, the year Higginbottom won the Rothschild Gold Cup at Nice.

The roofless shell of the 1835 engine house belonging to the Old Mine, photographed in 1861. Below are objects found in the Great Orme mines in 1969, including gunpowder horns, a lead pipe still containing straw fuses, and rounded beach stones that had been used as hammers

The King's Head, where modern Llandudno was conceived in 1846, was also the focal point of the old village that grew astride the simplest path from the sea to the plateau atop the Great Orme, where there was extensive Stone Age development. Today we know this path as Old Road, which commences as a hill opposite Christ Church in Llewelyn Avenue. Christ Church was built in 1857 and was embellished ten years later with the town's best steeple, which was demolished in 1975. As we start to walk up the hill we see a short road on the left where some delightful 1829 houses are dwarfed by a nine-storey block of flats completed during 1974, the product of a planning aberration in the dying days of Llandudno Urban District Council and Caernarvonshire County Council. This is Water Street, which takes its name from an ancient well and a steam engine erected in the early 1860s to pump the water into a reservoir in the Happy Valley.

Crossing Church Walks (described in the next chapter) we see the bottom terminus of the Great Orme Railway on the left. Its name, Victoria Station, is taken from Llandudno's first three-storey house, the Victoria, built by a Georgian mine agent and demolished in 1901 when work commenced on the 3 ft 6 ins (1m) gauge part-funicular cable-hauled tramway to the summit. The bottom section, 825 yards (754m) long, was opened on 31 July 1902, and the upper section 850 yards (777m) was completed on 8 July 1903, for the Whitsun holiday.

On the right there is a narrow cul-de-sac known as Tŷ Coch Road, after the original Tŷ Coch farm (now No.4) where a French refugee, Marcus le Louis, set up a school for the Llandudno New Mine Company, soon after the Battle of Waterloo. He stayed for four years, lodging at Pwllygwichiaid. It was in this road, part of which has been known as King William Street (after its inn of that name) and Mount Pleasant, that the Tŷ Gwyn Mine Company had their offices, smithy and carpenters' shop. The street also housed the town's first lock-up, built in 1855 for the newly appointed Inspector of Nuisances. It was a low building with two heavy oak doors and no windows, located behind 67 Church Walks.

The King's Head, named after William IV, is on the left, with an early 20th century extension at one end – the original doorway, now built up, can still be seen inside. One of its most famous licensees was "Professor" Walter Beaumont, 1898-1911. He used to give diving exhibitions from the pier, and from 1895 to 1909 gave spectacular underwater displays in a glass-sided tank in the Egyptian Hall, on the Pier. In May 1903 the town gave him an illuminated scroll thanking him for saving 113 people from drowning off Llandudno beach. His daughter Alice, who joined the act when she was only six, married Belgian violinist Henri Verbrughen, from the Pier orchestra. On 16 May 1964, their daughter Gabriel Woodward, of Las Vegas, had the unique experience of returning to her native town and the Pier she knew so well aboard the luxury cruise liner *Kungsholm,* for a six-month holiday with her aunt, Maud Deacon, at St. Margaret's Drive, Craig-y-don.

Behind the King's Head we find the old village square, once known as Tanyberllan, meaning "beneath the orchard," but now called Llwynonn Gardens. This was the traditional meeting place where statutory and mining proclamations were read, as were such newspapers as found their way to Llandudno during the Napoleonic wars.

The Square leads westwards into Cwlach Street, once the main shopping centre, past a sturdy stone building erected in 1837 as Caersalem Welsh Wesleyan Chapel and later converted into Dr. George Roberts's grammar school. Over the blocked-up doorway an inscribed slate tablet tells us: "The Right Honourable William Morris Hughes, Premier of Australia 1916-23, was educated in this building."

Cwlach Street has a short spur, known as Cwlach Road, leading to Haulfre Gardens which David Lloyd George, the local MP, opened as a public park in 1929. The gardens were developed between 1871 and 1876 by the then owner of the house, Henry Pochin, creator of the more famous Bodnant Gardens in the Conwy Valley. An early owner of the house was the teenage future baronet Thomas Johnstone Lipton. Born in a tenement, he left his native Glasgow as a boy, to work in America. Why he turned up at Llandudno is a mystery. He was still only 21 when he returned to Glasgow in 1871 to open the first of what became a national chain of Lipton's grocery shops, famous for their Lipton's Tea. He was a millionaire by 1880 and earned fame as a yachtsman who frequently competed in the Americas Cup. One of the owners after Pochin's departure was John Walker, of Osborne House (see Chapter 9, North Parade) until he died in 1913. Llandudno Urban District Council bought the estate for £5,000 in 1928.

In June 1980 Mrs. Margaret Moreland, a director of the Welsh National Opera, planted a tree in the garden, identified with a slate plaque, saying it commemorated the company's 25th visit to Llandudno (i.e. 1951 and 1957-80). Llandudno Urban Council passed into history in the 1974 reorganisation of local government and their cherished Haulfre Gardens fell into decay. There was a £280,000 restoration scheme in 1998, funded by the National Lottery, but residents were less than happy with the result – Councillor Tom Hannon going on record to say: "It is not what I envisaged. These gardens were one of Llandudno's premier attractions and in my opinion they have been ruined. They have taken out many of the well-established plants and shrubs and replaced them with colourless alternatives. It is simply awful." Invalids' Walk, a delightful path leading to the West Shore, commences beside the gate to Haulfre Gardens – one of its most famous regular users being Alice Liddell, of *Wonderland* fame.

Resuming our journey up Old Road, from the village square, we see an open space on the left, being the garden of Beaver Lodge. This was where the Miners' Arms used to stand. It was a low 18th century building with three dormer windows. On the opposite side of the hill 19 & 20 Old Road (formerly 1 & 2 Tŷ Newydd Cottages) sported the last thatched roof in Llandudno up to 1920.

Llandudno's first Post Office was opened in October 1838 at Greenhill, 18 Old Road, when Mrs. Ann Jones was appointed Receiver "under the guarantee of the inhabitants" of a Penny Post from Conwy. It was not until 21 January 1839 that Llandudno's first postmark was authorised – a two-line stamp inscribed *Llandudno Penny Post*, initially without a frame although the Post Office proof book contains a framed specimen of the same date. It was again entrusted to Mrs. Jones and her daughters. Letters were carried by a Conwy man, John Hughes, who used to walk across the West Shore sand dunes each day to work in the mines, returning in the evening with the letters. After the introduction of postage stamps in 1840, and numeral obliterators four years later, Llandudno was eventually allocated the cancellation *B47* (not to be confused with Bangor's earlier 47).

An old limestone drinking fountain in the wall on the right has run dry but it used to collect a continuous trickle of water from a spring in the garden of Westminster House, Tabor Hill – a road junction a little higher up. This junction was the scene of a tragedy in August 1932 when the original alloy steel drawbar on the 40-seat tramcar No.4 snapped, rather like a chocolate bar, as the descending car reached the top of the 1-in-4 hill. The car accelerated to an alarming speed and brakeman Edward Harris, aged 35, decided to jump off the front plat-

Some Great Orme houses: Wyddfyd (above) photographed in 1987, and the Farm Inn of J.Roberts, photographed in 1890.

form, taking with him 11-years-old Margaret Worthington who was returning to town after delivering a mid-day meal to her father at the Half-Way Station engine house. As they jumped, the car left the rails and they were both crushed against the wall and killed. Fifteen passengers were injured and the then owners of the trams were forced into liquidation.

Without knowing anything about the 1932 accident, Arthur Reginald Ellison, the resident engineer in charge of the construction of the tramway, was 87 years of age, when (having retired to Llandudno from working abroad) he told the author in 1963 how he had fooled the Government inspector, Colonel Von Donop, during the commissioning brake test in 30 July 1902. There were two braking systems on each car, one to come into operation automatically if the rope went slack, the other a manual system. Contrary to appearances, the overhead trolley on the cars has nothing to do with powering the system – it is a telephone link to the Half-Way Station powerhouse. Just to ensure the hand-wound emergency brakes appeared to work Mr. Ellison arranged with the powerhouse to stop the system as soon as they received a brief ring on the phone. "Colonel Von Donop said STOP! and while the brakeman began to wind down the four slipper brakes I flicked the dynamo handle to operate the telephone, unseen by the Inspector who was duly impressed with the result," recalled Mr. Ellison – the young man seen on the roof of Car No.4 in commemorative photographs taken on that day. Next day the line was opened to the public and by the end of December had carried 76,000 passengers.

Bryn Tabor, at 3 Tabor Hill, was taken over by Sir Sidney Harmer, Director of Natural History at the British Museum, for his observation post during the total eclipse of the sun on 29 June 1927, when Llandudno was at the centre of the narrow belt affected.

At the top of Old Road, on the left, Llwynonn Terrace marks the site of Hen Dafarn (i.e. Old Tavern), the village's original 17th century alehouse. It was in the yard of this tavern that the Baptists claim to have introduced Nonconformity to Llandudno in 1798. Near here a gold coin belonging to the Attrebates, a tribe which lived in the Thames Valley in the 1st century BC, was dug up in 1924 – the first Early Iron Age coin to be discovered in North Wales. The four cottages making up Llwynonn Terrace formed a school for many years, run by different people from about 1864 until World War One, the last owner being Louisa Eakin, whose brother-in-law C.J.Montgomery opened Tanybryn School, in Tanybryn Road.

Several roads radiate from the top of Old Road, among them Wyddfyd Road beside a rock shelf with the hybrid name of Tan-y-stage where Twm o'r Nant is said to have performed one of his famous interludes in 1761 – Llandudno's first record of a theatrical production. Along this road there are still remains of stone pens where a sheep fair used to be held annually on 22 September, until the people lost their common land in 1848. Opposite the picturesque Wyddfyd Cottage, with its incongruous palm tree, there is a footpath on to the headland known as Pen-y-dinas where, among the remains of a prehistoric hill-fort, there is a large altar-like stone that can be rocked by hand (despite statements that it is now immovable). Seemingly a natural phenomenon, it was once believed to have druidic associations and was used by the Welsh bards in the proclamation ceremony for their 1864 Eisteddfod.

Another of the roads radiating from the top of Old Road leads to the summit, via a notoriously steep 1-in-4 hill in front of Belle Vue Terrace. Many a modern driver who fails to get into first gear in good time finds this hill difficult, although a Mercedes was driven up it as long ago as September 1903, by Gerald Higginbotham who, in the same year, won the Rothschild gold cup at Nice. It was the first motorcar to make the journey. A Stockport motorcyclist who made a noisy and unsuccessful attempt to ride up Old Road in June 1914 was fined £1 for endangering the public.

Behind Belle Vue Terrace a narrow farm road leads to Llandudno's last readily recognisable cromlech, or Stone Age burial chamber – known for countless decades as Lletty'r Filiast (i.e. lodging house of the greyhound bitch). It comprises four upright stones about 4 ft high (1.2m), which support the remains of a big capstone. There are also two detached portions of the capstone. The chamber stands at the excavated and robbed end of an oval mound that would have been 80 ft (24m) long. The remains of two similar chambered tombs are known on the Orme. Two early chapels, long since closed, are readily recognisable in this area, Horeb (1860) in Cromlech Street, and Hyfrydle (1893) in St. Beuno's Road.

The Summit road crosses a cattle-grid onto the plateau. To the right are the quarries that supplied some of the stone for Conwy suspension bridge, completed in 1826. Half-Way Station is nearby, dividing the Great Orme Railway into two cable-hauled sections. The station was rebuilt during 2001. As well as being an exchange station for passengers to walk between the upper and lower section cars, this is also the winding house for both sections. It was steam operated from 1902 until 1958 when it was converted to electricity. Many people are puzzled by the numbering of the four cars, 4 and 5 on the bottom section, and 6 and 7 on the top. Originally No.1 was designed for carrying coal to the steam-driven Half-Way station and coffins for funerals at St.Tudno's cemetery; Nos. 2 and 3 were short cars for off-peak use.

Opposite Half-Way Station is a 3,800-years-old copper mine, which was opened to the public in 1991. Remains of centuries of copper ore extraction, including some very deep shafts, are to be found at various points on the Great Orme, and intrepid tourists were being taken into prehistoric sections as long ago as the 1840s, but these very ancient workings were unknown until the 1980s.

In 1976 an amateur caving archaeologist found two big galleries from which artefacts could be carbon dated to before 1020 BC. Soon afterwards the local authority was given a land reclamation grant to remove a large unsightly mound of mining spoil, in which there was a deep hole fenced off with nothing more secure than chicken wire. With archaeologists keeping an eye on the job it was not long before the oldest known copper mines in Europe were discovered, dating from about 1800 BC. They form a site of major international significance to students of the Bronze Age, and these are what have been opened to the public.

A coin of the Emperor Vespasian (AD 68-79) dug up on the Great Orme in 1890.

There are about three miles (5km) of tunnels, through which a shorter convenient route has been mapped out for tourists. From these tunnels visitors can gaze in wonder into large worked-out chambers to which the only access is through holes that could have been negotiated only by children. It is thought the Llandudno mines were abandoned with the advent of the Iron Age, and may have remained closed during nearly five centuries of Roman occupation (although two large hoards of Roman coins have been found in the area). They were reopened in the 17th century and worked until a few years after the 1848 abolition of import duty on cheaper Australian and North and South American copper ore, from when British mining declined rapidly.

Beyond the mines the road forks either to the summit, straight ahead, or to St.Tudno's Church, to the right (see Chapter 10, Marine Drive & Great Orme). From 1800 to 1861 the summit housed a semaphore telegraph station. The first station was a wooden hut and signalling mast erected by the Admiralty during the Napoleonic Wars, for communication between Point Lynas and Liverpool. The badly damaged hut was patched up in 1827 to form part of a Liverpool Docks Committee chain of twelve semaphore stations linking Holyhead to Liverpool, to give the city's merchants first news of sightings of ships that had been at sea for weeks or

Drawn in 1889, Victoria Inn and farm, home of the Brookes family in Church Walks, was demolished in 1902 to make way for Victoria tram station. The beam engine (below) served the Great Orme mines until 1857, when it was sold to Broughton Colliery. The gold service medal of the Llandudno Volunteers was awarded to Henry Lewis in 1801.

months with no knowledge of their fate. On a good day, using a system of numeric codes, a message could be relayed from Holyhead to Liverpool in ten minutes.

The Docks Committee initiative produced an early example of land grabbing by the Mostyn family. In September 1826 the Committee agreed to pay the Lord of the Manor of Gogarth, i.e. the Bishop of Bangor, £2 a year rent for the lease of the site, but Sir Thomas Mostyn stepped in and said it was his land. Some years after Sir Thomas's death in 1831, it was established that the Bishop was the rightful owner and he was refunded the lost rent. The Llandudno station was rebuilt in 1840 to a common pattern – examples of which can still be seen on Puffin Island (derelict) and at Llysfaen (occupied). The semaphore gave way to electric telegraph in 1861 and the Great Orme station closed in 1863.

Once holidaymakers discovered the new resort of Llandudno, and began exploring the Great Orme, Job Jones, most famous of the station keepers (1849-61), opened a tearoom on the premises. After the Liverpool Docks Committee gave up the building it opened as the Telegraph Beer House, and was still in operation until taken over as a temporary clubhouse for a new 18-hole golf course laid out in 1909. It gave way to the nine-bedroom Telegraph Hotel forming part of the golf course. This was requisitioned for use as a Royal Air Force radar station in 1941. Job Jones moved to 4 Charlton Street, where he died in 1896, aged 88, his wife Susannah having died in 1889, aged 82. They were all living at the lighthouse when their daughter Jane died in 1877, aged 36 – her sister Mary surviving until 1904.

In 1952 the hotel was bought by Leslie T. Salts and Randolph Turpin who, in the previous year, beat Sugar Ray Robinson to become Britain's first middleweight boxing champion for 60 years. Alterations were made to the building, which reopened in 1953 as the Summit Complex, incorporating an open-air boxing ring for demonstrations by Turpin, who was the resident licensee. The two men quarrelled some six years later and Turpin ran the business himself until 1961 when, after being served with an Income Tax writ for £16,000 dating back to his boxing days, he sold out to Llandudno Urban Council, who made further structural alterations. Turpin shot himself in 1966 when 37 years of age. The building was damaged by fire on 7 November 1985, by which time it had become the practice to keep it closed during the winter months.

The radio mast on the 679 ft (207m) summit was erected by the BBC in 1965 as a television relay link. Other systems have since been attached to the mast, including the Classic FM regional transmitter which began operating on 22 January 1996, when the author made the opening broadcast in a day of inaugural programmes from a temporary studio at Llandudno. In 1934 the same site was surveyed by the BBC as a potential location for their Welsh Region medium wave 10 kW Marconi transmitter that subsequently went to Penmon, in Anglesey, where it opened on 1 February 1937. Nearby there is an Ordnance Survey trig point, No, S1627.

Extremely strong winds can be experienced at the summit of the Great Orme. In October 1917 a gust of wind blew over tramcar No.7, weighing about 7 tons, while it was parked outside the shed at the summit. The same thing happened on 22 September 1922. Twenty people were taken to hospital after a theoretically impossible accident on 30 April 2000, when two trams collided head-on on the top section – prompting a major refurbishment of the system. The rival cabinlift (aerial cable car) transport system also terminates at the summit. The other station is a mile away, at the Happy Valley.

There is now a very good Visitor Centre beside the Summit Station – its exhibits include the old lighthouse lantern. There are some spectacular views from the summit, embracing the Conwy Valley, Snowdonia, Menai Strait, Anglesey, Isle of Man, Cumberland mountains, Lancashire shore, Liverpool Bay and contiguous Welsh coast.

The 1837 chapel in Cwlach Street became Llandudno Grammar School where William Morris Hughes was educated, later to become Prime Minister of Australia and member of Lloyd George's War Cabinet. The hat and chair he used in old age for ANZAC day parades are still preserved at a Sydney bank.

CHURCH WALKS   5

Church Walks is the elegant road that runs from the Pier entrance to the West Shore, completing the circuit around the Orme. It was a natural overflow development from the old village when it became necessary to build St. George's church (1840) as a replacement for St. Tudno's. The Pier end of the road was then a busy industrial centre, complete with 15 ft (4.5m) diameter water wheel on the site of the house named Min-y-don, at the junction of North Parade and Church Walks. Used for operating a hammer, to crush the ore which was here brought out of the mountain on a tramway, the wheel was driven by a continuous river pumped out of the mines. The house known as The Stowe, at No.67, was built in 1857, and has some unusual interior features. It was once used as offices by the Tŷ Gwyn Mining Company. There were two powerful Cornish steam engines, one behind the present Empire Hotel (where its tall chimney survived until 1969).

The other engine was beside the present hotel, in Tŷ Gwyn Road, on what is now a small parking area to the right. This is the site of a house that carried the unusual name of Tŷ Aildro, meaning "house for the second time," until its demolition in March 1977. The house was built in 1864 as the first Turkish baths in Wales, offering facilities for six bathers. Four years later it was serving as a Roman Catholic chapel when Father Patrick Mulligan, aged 34, arrived, charged with the melancholy mission of closing a district that stretched from Rhyl to Bangor, and southwards as far as Dolgellau, but had only 27 worshippers. He stayed for 38 years and opened the present Catholic church in Lloyd Street in 1893 – when Tŷ Aildro returned to domestic use and was given its name. In the 1881 census Father Mulligan was shown as living "in the flat below the Roman Catholic Chapel (St. Mary's)." He died in 1906, and was buried on the Great Orme – where his grave was vandalised in 1983.

A little higher up Tŷ Gwyn Road, in the garden of the house known as Ardwy Orme (built in 1895), a glazed building resembling a garden shed is really a facade for Thomas Kendrick's Cave. It takes its name from a lapidary (a stone polisher) who used to earn a living making jewellery for tourists out of stones collected from the beach. In 1880 he decided to try to enlarge his natural workshop by removing rubble from the rear. It proved to be an ancient man-made wall, sealing off a long curving cave, 50 ft (15m) long (with a dangerous floor-level hole, on the right, near the end, leading to a drop of unknown depth) in which were found four human skeletons among remains of the extinct British cave bear and our first primitive cow (bos longifrons) of some 10,000 years ago. A horse jawbone had been carved with chevrons and is preserved in the Stone Age gallery of the British Museum. There were also some flint fragments. Some of the discoveries, including the bones of bos longifrons and two bear teeth perforated and incised for use as jewellery, were bought by the Llandudno Library Committee for £120 in 1902. They were displayed in glass cases until 1968, when, during the winding up of Llandudno Field Club (founded in 1906, and to whom the items never belonged), the Librarian loaned them to a Rhos-on-sea man for safe custody in his private museum. Their whereabouts no longer seems to be known. Four carved front foot bones of roe deer found by Kendrick have survived and in 1996 were carbon dated to the Ice Age of about 12,000 years ago, suggesting there were two quite separate ancient occupations of the cave. Thomas Kendrick died on Boxing Day 1897, aged 76.

The Empire Hotel was built in 1854 as the town's first modern block of shops (chemist, grocer and Italian warehouse) all run by an enterprising 23-years-old Denbigh man named Thomas Williams. In his *Visitor's Hand-Book,* published in 1855, Williams advertised such varied commodities as gunpowder, bathing caps, fresh German leeches, fire insurance, Black Draught family medicine, and Llandudno Bouquet perfume. Although bearing the name of the Rev. Richard Parry as author, and often described as the town's first guidebook, it was but a thinly disguised reprint of Owen Williams's brochure (except for the erroneous substitution of April for August as the month of the auction). As the Empire Hotel the building was reconstructed internally in 1904, the front was extended at ground level in 1969, there were considerable extensions to the rear during 1967-69, and again in 1979-80, and the pillared front porch was added in 1993. The four pillars, which were bought at a Sotheby's auction, were given by Queen Victoria to the Winter Gardens, at St. Leonards-on-sea. This was the hotel used by the Lewis Carroll Society for their highly successful 1999 summer seminar.

The narrow cul-de-sac beside the Empire, usually known as Tan-yr-ogof (meaning beneath the cave, i.e. Kendrick's Cave) was where Britain's famous Codman Punch & Judy tradition was nurtured after Richard Codman was banned from the Promenade, two months after his first performance in May 1864. He eventually returned to the Promenade but he and his son Herbert continued to perform at Tan-yr-ogof until about 1920.

Continuing past the cul-de-sac, one arrives at an impressive residential block that formed the administrative hub of the new resort. Bella Vista, at No. 72, was leased in 1866 by the town's first bank, the National Provincial Bank of England, which had provided a twice-weekly agency since 1861 at Mrs. Flanagan's boarding house at 1 Moelfre View, now 123 Mostyn Street. In 1988 this house became a detached annexe of the Empire Hotel. Capri, at No. 70, was our first Town Hall, from 1854 until 1902. This was where the town's first magistrates' court was held in 1856 – transferred from Conwy because of the large number of summonses issued against Llandudno residents who refused to pay their first town rate demand of half-a-crown ($12\frac{1}{2}$ p) in the pound, levied in 1855 to meet a total local government budget of £1,007. Here, too, the Llandudno Association for the Prosecution of Felons was formed in 1857 (in the absence of a police force), as a club that offered rewards for information leading to convictions. After a brief period as a grocery shop Bryn Arfon, at No. 68, became the offices of the Llandudno Water & Gas Company in 1856. The town's first gas works was opened in 1857 and the first forty street lamps were illuminated in 1860. Bronwendon, at No. 63, marks the site of the town's first supermarket, William Prichard's Shop founded in 1831. Llandudno had no doctor in those days and Mrs. Prichard used to supply medicines to match any ailment – all out of six bottles labelled tincture of rhubarb, castor oil, paregoric elixir (alcohol and opium), oppodildo, spirits of nitre and laudanum.

On the opposite corner Ormeside, at No. 19, was built in 1879 as Gouldings Hotel, on the site of the George & Dragon Inn dating back to the beginning of the nineteenth century. The shippons of the George & Dragon are still standing at the rear and they were used until 1916 when the last town dairy closed. Mr. Goulding used to advertise: "Doors, piano and gas closed at 11 p.m. Gong sounds at 8 a.m." The building subsequently became a hostel for the staff of the Grand Hotel.

Proceeding across Old Road one finds at the corner, on the left, a house called Clovelly. This was the scene of a murder on the last night of 1991, some fifteen minutes before the New Year. A 44-years-old taxi driver stabbed his wife, who died on the pavement in Old Road, and injured five other residents, two very seriously. He then drove off in a car and killed himself and three others when he crashed at speed, seemingly deliberately, into the front of an oncoming car at Talycafn, in the Conwy Valley.

Bodlondeb Castle is an imposing building on the right of Church Walks. Although it has been a Methodist holiday home since 1931, it was requisitioned for use as a military hospital during World War One, and was a private school before that, initially all boys, and from 1910 all girls. Residents have usually called it Davies's Folly ever since it was built in 1897. Created at enormous cost by Thomas P. Davies, son of the founder of St. George's Hotel, it incorporates many tons of imported marble, with translucent pillars on the stairway. Its stained glass windows illustrate the arms of the royal tribes of Wales. No one – not even his family – ever ascertained what he intended doing with such a splendid place.

Opposite stands the Royal Hotel and Mostyn Arms. The entire building was once called Mostyn Arms, when built as the town's first major hotel. The name was changed because of confusion with another Mostyn Arms beside Llanrhos church, in the neighbouring parish. One of its most notable guests was the Rev. C. H. Spurgeon, in June 1862, when he preached to an open-air gathering on the site of 15 Bodhyfryd Road (Myrtle Villa). In 1979 the name Mostyn Arms was revived for an extension beside the Royal Hotel.

Until the death of the owner, William Barrow, in 1972, the house known as Nant-y-glyn, at 59 Church Walks, contained a nationally famous collection of musical antiquities. It was here that Alfred Einstein tracked down the autographed last missing page of Mozart's *Rondo in A Major* (K386) which became scattered all over Europe in 1791, and which was given its world premiere at Vienna in 1958 – with the aid of a photograph of the Llandudno page.

The Rectory, hidden behind a high wall, has known three incumbents named John Morgan. The last was actually born there, in 1886, while his father (of the same name) was the Rector – in immediate succession to the first John Morgan who was the last of Llandudno's

An 1864 photograph showing the unfinished roof of the Eisteddfod pavilion in Upper Mostyn Street. The building in the centre foreground, in front of St. George's church, is the Ship Inn.

perpetual curates, 1857-60, and the first resident Rector, 1860-85. The third John Morgan was appointed to the living in 1933 but left in the following year to become Bishop of Swansea & Brecon, and eventually Archbishop of Wales.

St. George's church, designed by John Welch, of Conwy, was consecrated in 1840, having been paid for largely by anonymous contributions from the brothers Archibald and William Worthington, lessees of the Old Mine. It can seat 450 people. The clock in the West Tower was added in memory of the Reverend Edward Thomas Evans, who had been the resident perpetual curate for six years when he died on a visit to Rome on 21 April 1857, aged 33. In 1864 Dean Liddell, who used to lead his family and servants to St. George's Church, complained to Rector John Morgan about the clock's bad timekeeping. The Rector, who also happened to be chairman of the Town Commissioners (1861-66), suggested the Commissioners should each pay 6d or 1s a year to maintain the clock, although he added: "It does not matter, perhaps, what time it keeps for ourselves when the visitors have gone, as we do not have much to do then." In the absence of radio, timekeeping was then a haphazard business, and the Llandudno sunrise was 15 minutes and 20 seconds later than in London.

St. George's was designated the parish church by Queen Victoria in Council, at Osborne House, on 18 November 1862, and retains this distinction until September 2002, when the church will be closed to concentrate the town's dwindling congregations in Holy Trinity Church (which will take over the role of parish church).

Continuing down the road we come to the former St. George's National School, opened in 1846, and extended in 1854 just in time for an inspection by the notorious Commissioners of Inquiry into the State of Education in Wales. They reported that the only master, at £21 a year, was a 25-years-old former farmer whose knowledge of English was deficient. Children provided their own copybooks and paid fees of a penny a week. The school closed in 1993 but reopened in the autumn with 200 pupils in a new church-aided building near Loreto Convent, preserving the old name of St. George, but in Welsh: Ysgol San Siôr. The Llandudno Seaside Buildings Preservation Trust was set up to raise money with which they hope to convert the original National School into a community centre.

The enclosed land within the junction of Church Walks and Abbey Road is known as John Bright's Paddock, a reminder that the great Victorian statesman kept a horse here for his frequent visits to the town. The houses opposite occupy the site of a limekiln and a well, hence the old name of Ffynnon-yr-odyn for this area. Plas Gogarth old people's home was the town's first Parsonage.

Proceeding into Abbey Road, towards West Shore, one finds Loreto Convent, founded in 1919 on the last traces of Tŷ Draw farm. It incorporated a school under the auspices of the sisters of the Institute of the Blessed Virgin Mary, until the last of its elements – the boarding school – closed in 1970. Princess Bejerana, of Siam, was a day pupil during World War Two. The former school hall, which had become a conference centre run by the convent, was seriously damaged by an arsonist on 21 December 1985.

Juxtaposed opposite the convent, on one of the gateposts of Brookfield Mansions, at 85 Abbey Road, is the Devil's head, substituted for a rose by Isaac Owens, a stonemason who, towards the end of his contract, was in dispute with the builder. His revenge went unnoticed for many years although it is now obvious with its features picked out in red paint.

Profile House, at 33 Abbey Road, was named by Leslie Leach, the last silhouette artist of the Welsh piers when he retired in 1969, aged 70. Using only a scissors and three layers of black paper he produced over a million profiles. He took over the Llandudno kiosk from "Major" Harry Lawrence Oakley, MBE, ARCA, a regular contributor to *Bystander Magazine,* whose clients had included the Duke of Windsor, as Prince of Wales. He had served as a captain in the Green Howards, and had worked as a silhouettist in Yorkshire and Shropshire before settling in Llandudno.

Bryn Rosa, 16 Abbey Road, displays a slate plaque, supplied by the author in 1987, recording that it was the boyhood home of William Morris Hughes, who became Prime Minister of Australia. He was born in London, of Welsh parents, on 25 September 1864, and was four years of age when sent to live with an aunt at Llandudno. He spent the rest of his boyhood and early youth at Bryn Rosa until he left to spend a short period as a pupil teacher at St.Stephen's School, Westminster. He emigrated to Australia in 1884. There he became a leading trade union organiser and was elected to the New South Wales Parliament in 1894. The formation of the Australian Federation in 1901 broadened his political horizon and resulted in his becoming Prime Minister in 1915. He revisited Llandudno in August 1916 when in London as a member of David Lloyd George's War Cabinet, and during a civic reception at the Town Hall reminisced about his youth with former school contemporaries, adding that he had revisited his old home and his old school. His last visit was in 1921, when he and his wife spent a few days at St.George's Hotel, for him to unveil the Lloyd George statue in Caernarfon's Castle Square. During that visit he stood outside Bryn Rosa for several minutes, reminiscing with his wife, watched from a window by the occupant, Mrs. Annie Pritchard. "He never knocked on the door and as he walked away he turned round for one last look," Mrs. Pritchard told the author.

Billy Hughes, affectionately known as The Little Digger, died in 1952. It had been the custom for him to take the salute in Martin Place, Sydney, at each annual parade of ex-servicemen on Anzac Day (25 April), when he would wear the distinctive Australian soldier's slouch hat given to him by the Gallipoli veterans. In old age he was provided with a chair from the head office of the Commonwealth Bank of Australia. After his death the chair was still brought out of the bank, with his slouch hat hanging on the back, adorned with a sprig of rosemary. This custom continued until the parade had to take a different route in 1974 because of excavations for a new underground station, and the conversion of Martin Place into a pedestrianised zone. A plaque has been placed on the bank wall to commemorate the ceremony – and the hat is still preserved in the bank's vaults. William Hughes was featured on an Australian postage stamp in 1972.

Maes Gwyn, 46 Abbey Road, was the home of County Court Registrar James Jones Marks, and later of his grandson Brigadier John Mark Herbert-Roberts, who married Nicola Lechmere-Macaskie. Brigadier Roberts became a devout Roman Catholic convert and named all his ten children after saints. Four sons became officers in the Brigade of Guards: Hilarion Lechmere Roberts (Welsh Guards, who survived injuries aboard the *Sir Galahad* in the Falklands War, but died in a road accident) and Sebastian, Cassian and Fabian, of the Irish Guards, who made history in February 1996 when all three led the changing of the guard at Buckingham Palace, with Sebastian John Lechmere Roberts commanding the 1st Battalion Irish Guards (and later promoted brigadier). Daughter Helena married the Welsh Guards adjutant who was among those trapped on the *Sir Galahad,* and makes her home in Abbey Road. Captain Fabian Roberts was the officer in charge of the pallbearers at the funeral of Queen Elizabeth, the Queen Mother, in April 2002.

Bron Heulog, 2 Abbey Road, was the pre-marriage home of novelist Edith Nepean, who died in March 1960, age 84. She was educated at St.George's School and studied art under Robert Fowler, three of whose works are displayed at the Gogarth Abbey Hotel. She wrote 35 novels between 1917 and 1958, nearly all on a Welsh theme. Although her married home was at Ealing Common she spent long holidays at Llandudno, and even into her 70s could often be seen swimming in the sea off the West Shore. She was buried on the Great Orme.

Llandudno in 1855. Pwll-y-gwichiaid farm is still in existence and the engine chimney of the Tŷ Gwyn mine is belching smoke from the site of what is now the Empire Hotel garage. The farm had been replaced by South Parade in the photo below but the luggage porter's hut was still on the beach.

"It was thought that I was most extravagant in laying out the belt of land for a promenade as it was considered a waste of property," reminisced Owen Williams at the turn of the last century. By that time the two-mile (3km) sweep of Llandudno's northern shore had become renowned as an example of good planning. "If I had had my own way it would have been deeper," added Williams. However in 1854 the planning of the slowly growing town was taken out of his hands and vested in a Charing Cross firm of architects, Messrs. Wehnert & Ashdown – and Owen Williams moved on to design Rhyl and Trearddur Bay.

To the eternal confusion of residents and visitors alike, Llandudno promenade has a different street name for each block of buildings. The obelisk-shaped War Memorial, designed by Sidney Colwyn Foulkes, was unveiled in 1922 in Prince Edward Square, and visited in the following year by the Prince of Wales (the future King Edward VIII who abdicated to become the Duke of Windsor). It lists 219 victims of World War One and another 122 who fell in World War Two, their names on four plaques added in 1957.

Commencing at the cenotaph we have South Parade, once the farmland of Pwllygwichiaid, meaning "pool of the periwinkles." It was a farm famous as the 1790 birthplace of Hugh Hughes, an artist and engraver who has been compared with Bewick, and who most famously published *The Beauties of Cambria,* a quarto book containing sixty woodcuts of his own work. At 11 years of age he started Llandudno's first Calvinistic Methodist Sunday school at the farm. Trevor Street and Tŷ Isa Road stand behind the modern facade to mark the eastern and southern boundaries of the former farm.

Hughes's mother Jane was from Meddiant, a farm at Glanconwy. His father Thomas was recorded in 1801 as churchwarden for Llandudno, indicating he was probably literate and able to speak English – unusual skills for that period. In 1814 Hugh Hughes took himself off to London, but when, in 1818, he put out a printed leaflet for *The Beauties of Cambria,* to be published in the following year by a Strand "bookseller to the Prince Regent, and the Duke and Duchess of York," he proclaimed himself to be "H.Hughes of Llandudno," a place few Londoners would ever have heard of. He added: "The Proprietor, aware of the ardent and generous love of the Fine Arts, which is diffused among the higher ranks of his countrymen, feels encouraged in thus presenting himself to their notice and soliciting their countenance to an arduous, but he trusts laudable, undertaking; he assures his Patrons that no pains shall be spared in the exercise of his talents; and hopes to prove, by the satisfaction his Work may afford, that the patronage of his Friends will not have been ill bestowed." An enlarged edition was published in 1822.

St. George's Hotel was opened in August 1854 as the first modern building on the promenade. Its remoteness was such that the deeds refer to the plot as being "near to the village of Llandudno." It was built by Isaiah Davies, an astute young man of 24 who was born at a farm on the Little Orme and who inherited the King's Head after marrying Ann Owens, daughter of the licensee and five years his senior, when he was only 19. His descendants used to claim he obtained the choice promenade site in exchange for cancelling the drinking debts at the King's Head of John Williams, agent to the Mostyn family, but he paid the average going rate of 1s.2½d (6p) a square yard (0.8sqm) for the lease of nearly 2,000 square yards (1872sqm).

Interestingly, the deed signatures of Isaiah Davies and John Williams were witnessed, on 30 October 1852, by Owen Williams, showing that the Liverpool surveyor maintained a prominent role in the early development of the resort he had envisaged. The hotel has since been extended several times. The water tower was added to accommodate and operate Llandudno's first lift. The long wing extending towards the town centre was erected in 1878 on the site of the hotel stables from where the town's first bus service (to Conwy railway station) began in 1856. The hotel's founding family company went into liquidation in March 1977. There is a three-light window in St. George's Church in memory of Isaiah Davies, who died on 10 November 1881, and his wife Anne Jane who died on 12 February 1896.

The new owner of the 90-bedroom St. George's Hotel was Michael Forte, who paid £250,000 for it in July 1977. Born in Italy in April 1913, he was the brother of Lord (Charles) Forte. The two brothers and their sister Anna, all from Monteforte, built up a series of major hotel and catering businesses, from humble beginnings with their 1934 opening of the Meadow Milk Bar, in London's Upper Regent Street. Mr. Forte sold the hotel in 1985. In the foyer of the St.George one can still see the original brass bell-knobs labelled *Boots, Ostler* and *Chambermaid* – knobs which were used by such famous guests as Napoleon III and his empress Eugénie, Bismarck, Disraeli, Dean Liddell, Gladstone, Churchill, Lloyd George and John Bright.

Trevone Hotel, at 10 St. George's Crescent, was Matthew Arnold's favourite Welsh holiday residence and it was here, in 1864, that he wrote his notes for his controversial *On the study of Celtic literature,* in which he recorded: "The best lodging-houses at Llandudno look eastward, towards Liverpool; and from that Saxon hive swarms are incessantly issuing, crossing the bay, and taking possession of the beach."

St. George's Crescent was completed in 1892 to fill the gap between the town's first seafront hotel and the Queen's Hotel, built by Owen Thomas in 1855, and outside which there is an interesting hexagonal Penfold letterbox of 1866, still providing a daily service.

The Imperial Hotel, at the eastern end of Gloddaeth Crescent, was created in 1872 by uniting a string of boarding houses of 1865. It was extended upwards at the beginning of the 20th century and again, after a serious fire on the top floor, during 1972. Its most famous guest was the exiled Queen Rambai Barni of Siam until she, like everyone else, was turned out in 1940 when the Imperial became the headquarters of Britain's evacuated Inland Revenue Department. (Queen Rambai Barni was subsequently allowed to return to Thailand, and died in Bangkok on 22 May 1984, aged 79). Future Prime Minister Jim Callaghan had an office at the Imperial for most of the war, and for six years he had a flat a few doors away at 7 Mostyn Crescent. He arrived as assistant secretary to the Inland Revenue Staff Federation, and also became billeting officer, filling most of the town's 400 hotels, and later the entertainment officer. His second daughter (Julia) was born at Llandudno Hospital. He was called up towards the end of the war for service with the Royal Navy. The 54th Philatelic Congress of Great Britain was held at the Imperial Hotel in 1972 – the first occasion for the Congress to visit Wales. A special branch Post Office was opened at the hotel for the event.

On the opposite corner of Vaughan Street one finds the Marine Hotel (originally the Adelphi), the scene of Llandudno's worst hotel fire, on 9 October 1920. It has the distinction of having been the home of Queen Elisabeth of Romania for five weeks in 1890, a visit which Llandudno will never be allowed to forget. Her parting words to the chairman of the Commissioners, describing Wales as a beautiful haven of peace, have been translated into Welsh for the town's official motto of "Hardd, Hafan, Hedd." Twenty-one top quality facsimiles of the letter were produced for each of the Commissioners, and these turn up from time to time. Streets have been named after her and shops boasted of her patronage for the next three-quarters of a century. Mostyn Street clockmaker W. Mayler celebrated his own retirement by having a bronze

ARCADIA THEATRE
LLANDUDNO

Cattin's Summer Follies

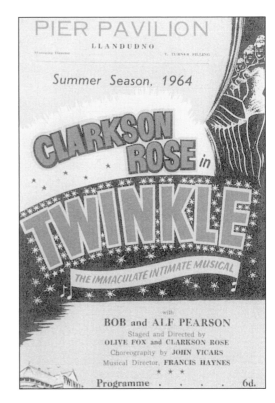

PIER PAVILION
LLANDUDNO

Summer Season, 1964

CLARKSON ROSE in

TWINKLE

THE IMMACULATE INTIMATE MUSICAL

with
BOB and ALF PEARSON
Staged and Directed by
OLIVE FOX and CLARKSON ROSE
Choreography by JOHN VICARS
Musical Director, FRANCIS HAYNES
★ ★ ★
Programme . . . . 6d.

1978

GRAND THEATRE

Llandudno Tel. 77327

Owner and General Manager: JOHN CREESE-PARSONS

SUMMER SERENADE OLDE TYME MUSIC HALL

starring ALEX MUNRO

★

NIGHTLY AT 8 pm
including SUNDAY

PIER & PAVILION
LLANDUDNO
General Manager & Secretary: T. TURNER PILLING

Farewell Programme

Codman's Punch & Judy booth has been a feature of Llandudno since 1864. For forty years another popular promenade entertainment was the bird circus of Gicianto Ferrari, who died in 1923.

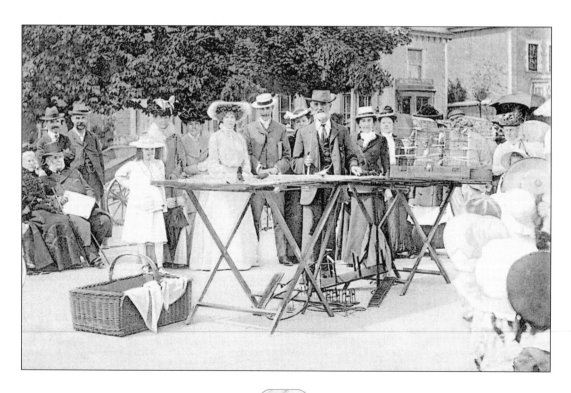

commemorative medal struck in honour of the Queen's visit (there was a specimen on display in one of the glass cases at Llandudno Library until 1964).

Queen Elisabeth was born in 1843, the daughter of Prince Hermann of Wied and Princess Marie of Nassau. In 1869 she married the future King Carol I of Romania (then spelt Roumania). She came to Llandudno by accident. Having written a novel about Wales, based on information gleaned in Bucharest, she decided to visit the Principality of her dreams. She asked Prince Ghyka, the Romanian Minister in London, to find her a remote spot for convalescence and contemplation. Prince Ghyka consulted Edward, the Prince of Wales who, remembering his visits of 1867 and 1880, provided Queen Elisabeth with his personal railway saloon, upholstered in silk, to convey her to Llandudno. Her initial reaction was open annoyance on finding herself at a busy holiday resort, but next morning Lord and Lady Mostyn called to see her at the hotel and in the afternoon she was driven to Gloddaeth for tea – the first of several visits. The Queen quickly warmed to Wales and a few days later went to the National Eisteddfod, at Bangor, where, at her request, the stage was decorated to look like a Welsh kitchen. During the eisteddfod she was admitted to the Gorsedd of Bards under her pen name of Carmen Sylva. She attended several concerts at Llandudno Pier Pavilion and went to such events as a children's party. She worshipped at Llanrhos Church and her tours took her to places as far afield as Caernarfon, Beaumaris, Llanberis and Capel Curig, and she was entertained at Penrhyn Castle, Baron Hill and Mostyn Hall.

She took frequent boat trips in the bay, declaring in her fluent English: "The only time my restlessness ceases is before the rolling waves." There was no jetty near the Adelphi Hotel and it became the practice for the boatman, William Lloyd Jones, to carry her across the shingle. With royal consent he changed the name of his boat to *Carmen Sylva* – and also gave the name to his house in Bodhyfryd Road (and was known to holidaymakers for the rest of his life as the Royal Boatman).

Writing from Llandudno to Baroness Deichmann (née Hilda de Bunsen, a childhood friend), Carmen Sylva said: "To tell you of all the kindness shown to me here is nearly impossible. It is a fairyland in every direction, and I am expanding like a dying plant under the first warm shower. For I was really half dead when I started my journey, in a piteous state of weakness and helplessness. Now I am getting up steam, and wind into sails, and begin to think perhaps I really have been a poet, and may be one again, not just a worthless wisp of straw. Here is paradise. I can only compare it to Lake Maggiore and the Corniche, climate, vegetation and all and I believe it is the very thing for me. I wanted just a little pleasure, to forget and forgive and look forward. The Mostyns have made their home lovely, I never saw kinder people in my life. Oh! how grateful I am to have come here,"

During her stay at Llandudno the Queen was visited at her hotel by the Prince and Princess Edward of Saxe-Weimar. The day before she was due to depart, most of the town's children paraded past her hotel, while she waved from a window. That evening the Pier Pavilion was filled to capacity for a farewell concert, at which she told a children's choir: "Your voices will always remain in my heart as a sweet farewell." Next day she was given an official send off by the town Commissioners and a royal salute of twenty-one lifeboat maroons was fired from the Great Orme, as she set off at 8 p.m. to join the night train to London – never to return. She died in 1916.

Soon after their return to Romania the Queen's faithful lady-in-waiting Hélène Vacaresco, who had been a popular figure at her side throughout her five weeks in Llandudno, was exiled by the King for becoming the mistress of Prince Ferdinand of Hohenzollern-Sigmaringen, destined to succeed Carol as King of Romania in 1922. Ferdinand was married in 1893 to Princess Marie, daughter of the Duke of Edinburgh (son of Queen Victoria). She too had a lover, for 30 years, writing: "Fidelity does not seem to have been decreed by nature." She was the second Romanian queen to tour North Wales, in 1925 when she also visited the National Eisteddfod.

The Hydro Hotel was opened in 1860 by a Dr. Norton of Chester, as the Llandudno Hydropathic & Winter Residence, but its progress was slow until 1872 when Dr. Henry Thomas, the son of a Caernarfon printer, took over. He was descended from Caernarfon's Coed Helen family. When the national registration of doctors was introduced, in 1858, the Medical Registrar refused to recognise Dr.Thomas's diploma of MD, awarded in 1855 by the Homeopathic Medical College of Pennsylvania. The correspondence dragged on for months, and included a letter from the college secretary, Dr. Charles J. Hempel, saying: "Dear Doctor Thomas, I am amazed by the boldness of your Registrar, who asserts that you have not furnished satisfactory evidence of your claims to a diploma of MD from one of the regularly chartered institutions of our country" - the letter adding that a certificate signed by a Philadelphia judge had been supplied to the British Registrar. The Medical Council told Thomas he would not be registered, but he could seek to have the ruling reversed by a court.

"This opinion I should have acted upon but for my solicitors informing me that the Medical Council, by traversing the case from court to court, could ruin me in pocket before a final decision could be obtained," said Henry Thomas. Instead he decided to continue describing himself as a doctor of medicine and Medical Superintendent of his establishment until his death in 1894, at the age of 62, and was never prosecuted.

At his Llandudno Hydropathic Establishment he offered a wide range of treatment including a "compressed air bath, which is especially beneficial in bronchial affections, weakness of the vocal organs and chronic catarrh." His equipment included an "American reactionary lifting machine, for health-lifts, or lifting cures," while his medicine chest contained arsenic, belladonna and Spanish fly.

In 1868 he published a shilling book of cures, followed in 1877 by an enlarged 587-page edition for just about any ailment one could think of. For instance, for a headache caused by "the abuse of ardent spirits, sedentary mode of life, and severe mental labour" he recommended four drops of either nux vomica or belladonna in a tumbler of water. One drop on the tongue of either of these hazardous chemicals was his cure for nightmares. Noting that diphtheria had first made its appearance in Britain in 1856, Dr. Thomas recommended a small measure of hydrochloric acid in water.

Henry Thomas also commissioned John Price, of Pwllycrochan (best known as author of *Old Price's Remains*) to write *Llandudno, and how to enjoy it*, published in 1874. Ostensibly a guidebook, it was full of praise for Henry Thomas's establishment, the only hotel mentioned in its 162 pages, and the only hotel permitted to advertise in a rear section that also advertised Edward Thomas's Homeopathic Pharmacy at 31 Bridge Street Row, Chester.

One of Henry Thomas's daughters, Dora Thomas, was the finder in a friend's collection of one of the world's most famous postage stamps, the Blue Mauritius specimen that was bought by King George V, and remains the gem of the Royal collection.

The 1,505-seat North Wales Theatre opened with a production of *Jesus Christ, Super Star* on 28 June 1994. It was officially opened by the Prince of Wales during a spectacular Royal Gala Concert on 3 July. It is one of the finest theatres in the country, with a proscenium 50 ft (15m) wide and 26 ft (8m) high. The available stage depth is 45 ft (14m) and there are 58 counter-weight line sets for flying scenery. Its birth was something of a planning miracle. The original concept was for an £11m leisure centre incorporating an opera house and a swimming pool. That plan was trimmed to £9.75m, for which a £5.8m Government subsidy was anticipated at a time when the Welsh Office was able to give £8.5m for commercial development in

Cardiff, £4.5m for two new hotels in Cardiff and Swansea, and £3m for a Cardiff Trade and Exhibition Centre. With nothing forthcoming for Llandudno, the plan was slashed to the present £4.5m North Wales Theatre, with maximum funding put into the auditorium and stage, resulting in a somewhat spartan front-of-house.

The theatre links up, internally, with the adjoining Conference Centre, also opened by the Prince of Wales on 27 October 1981, when he was accompanied by Diana, Princess of Wales, whom he had married in the July. At the subsequent reception Princess Diana told the author it was her first visit to the town. The main hall of the multipurpose Conference Centre can seat 1,200 delegates.

A speech made in this hall in 1987 by Labour Party leader Neil Kinnock found its way into a GCSE English textbook published by Oxford University Press in 1996. The occasion was what should have been a celebratory 50th anniversary conference of Labour Party Wales, on 15 & 16 May, but the event was reduced to an AGM because of the announcement that a general election would take place on 11 June. Addressing the meeting, Mr. Kinnock asked: "Why am I the first Kinnock to be able to get to university? Why is Glenys [his Holyhead-born wife, and future MEP] the first woman in her family in a thousand generations to be able to get to university? Was it because all our predecessors were thick? Did they lack talent – those people who could sing, and play and recite and write poetry; those people who could make wonderful, beautiful things with their hands; those people who could dream dreams, see visions; those people who had such a sense of perception as to know in times so brutal, so oppressive, that they could win their way out of that by coming together."

The speech was used in that year's General Election political broadcast for the Labour Party and was plagiarised that same year by a United States Democrat who made the same case for himself. Still known as "the Llandudno speech," it was chosen for the 1996 textbook as a lesson in speech making that relied on content and the power of personal experience rather than political rhetoric.

Next-door to the North Wales Theatre and contiguous Conference Centre stands the derelict Arcadia Theatre. It had 1,150 seats when it opened as the Victoria Palace in July 1894, being the first phase of a project that was to have included a pier. It was built by a company led by Jules Rivière, a 75-years-old eccentric musician who had fallen out with Llandudno Pier Company for whom he had come to the town as resident conductor. He opened with an orchestra of 42 musicians and two vocalists, one advertised as Mlle. Trebelli. Goodness knows who *she* was, for the famous mezzo-soprano Zélia Trebelli (a name made out of the reversal of Gillebert) had died in France two years earlier, and her singing daughter Antoinette Trebelli had by then changed her name to Antonia Dolores. Six years later Rivière was to fall out with the whole of Llandudno and move to the new Victoria Pier at Colwyn Bay, taking his orchestra with him. Nevertheless he has streets named after him in both towns and in 1895 his stature was such that Sir Charles and Lady Hallé gave a piano and violin recital with his orchestra. The name of his theatre changed, first to Rivière's Concert Hall, and after Rivière's departure, to the Llandudno Opera House in 1900, ready for a visit by the Carl Rosa Opera company who established a formidable reputation with a pioneering policy of touring all operas in the English language, for maximum entertainment of the maximum number of people. That philosophy is now overtaken by the elitist argument that real opera lovers want the authenticity of the original language, and the alleged wider field of international singers incapable of emulating the chorus by learning more than one language.

Later this theatre became the Hippodrome, and on Whit Saturday 1915, it entered its most famous phase as the Arcadia and the home of Will Catlin's Pierrots. The impresario once told the author of the day when Arthur Haynes, the comedian topping the bill, complained that his

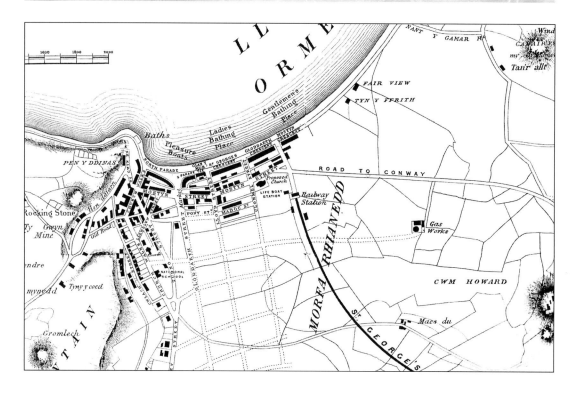

An 1864 plan of Llandudno shows no development south of Madoc Street, apart from the older section of Church Walks. The Llandudno lifeboat *Theodore Price* operated from 1902 to 1930 and saved 39 lives. The town's first motorised lifeboat arrived in 1932.

name was in the same sized letters as everyone else. The posters were changed immediately to read: "Will Catlin presents Catlin's Follies with an all star cast," an uncompromising formula which was retained for decades.

Will Catlin was 82 when he collapsed and died on Llandudno promenade in 1953, while walking to a matinee performance at his Arcadia. Catlin's Showtime carried on until 1968. Collectors of theatre memorabilia will have copies of "The Grand Final Programme," dated 23 September 1967. However, others will have what was printed a year later as the "Gala Farewell Programme," with the cryptic addition of the words: "Subject to slight alteration – or gross interference." Llandudno Urban Council had agreed to buy the Arcadia for £37,500 in 1967 but the Welsh Office, who controlled local government purse strings, had other ideas. Secretary of State for Wales George Thomas, later to become Speaker of the House of Commons, was persuaded to come to Llandudno to discuss the problem, and local MP Ednyfed Hudson Davies took him to the Arcadia to see the Catlin show. Much to everyone's surprise Cardiff comedian Wyn Calvin (whose brother was minister of the English Presbyterian Church, in Gloddaeth Street) made an impromptu and uncharacteristic political speech from the stage, pleading for the theatre's future. The controversy was great for business and the Arcadia takings for 1968 were 25% up on the previous year – and the valuation price of the theatre was increased to £41,500. The Welsh Office relented, the deal went through, and the Urban Council continued in the Catlin tradition until 1993.

Llandudno Sailing Club have their headquarters, built in 1968, next to the Arcadia. Their oldest trophy bears the inscription "Llandudno Regatta 1860" although the earliest records of a club are for 1895, and that club faded into obscurity with the outbreak of war in 1914. The present club was formed in 1960 and was host in 1969 for the Prince of Wales Cup race, held in Welsh waters for the first time in its long history, in honour of that year's investiture of the Prince of Wales at Caernarfon Castle.

Until 2001 there was a large open space between the Sailing Club and the Washington Hotel. This was known as Tŷ'n-y-ffrith, meaning "house in the sheep pasture." That was the name of an early pair of squatter's hovels that survived until October 1899, having been much elongated over the years so that it looked like a terrace of four dissimilar cottages and some outhouses. The owner, John Roberts, refused to relinquish his holding, established by long usage, at the time of the enclosure of the Common, but was persuaded to pay rent for it. His stand became part of the town's folklore, so that the original mud and thatch farm was eventually pointed out to tourists as the place where Llywelyn the Great hid from the soldiers of Henry III! The town's first Calvinistic Methodist sermon was preached here in 1806. In the end the occupiers were forced out as a health hazard, for their property was not connected to the town's sewer. The open land was used in June 1914 in conjunction with the *Daily Mail* seaplane that arrived in the bay, offering passenger flights at four guineas (£4.20) a time. The first taker was G.S.Yeoman, manager of the Craig-y-don Boarding House, now renamed the County Hotel. On the following day a well-known local suffragette, Miss May Jones, of The Bungalow, West Shore, became the first Llandudno woman to take to the air – having already made her mark as the first woman to drive a car in Birmingham. For many decades this land was a popular putting green for visitors, but a smart block of "assisted living" retirement flats, confusingly named Cwrt San Tudno (meaning St.Tudno's Court) was built on it during 2001-02.

The Washington Hotel has displayed a sign depicting George Washington on one side and the Capitol, in Washington D.C. on the other. It takes its name from the latter, because of its domed design, but the hotel contains a copy of a painting of the man, from the Congress Art Gallery, specially commissioned in 1966 by California Congressman James Corman.

For several years the County Hotel was run by world snooker champion Fred Davis and his wife Sheila. For nearly three decades brothers Fred and Joe Davis monopolised the world snooker titles. During Sheila Davis' incumbency the County Hotel was the home of an outstanding painting of Llandudno beach by Sydney Muschamp, dating from about 1878. However it had passed into the hands of a Sheffield owner by the time it was auctioned at Sotheby's in 1986 for £26,200.

The Dorchester, which opened on the seafront in 1937, was the last new hotel to be built at Llandudno. It was built for the parents of Sheila Davis, wife of snooker champion Fred. Before that they lived at the Sunnyside Hotel, in Llewelyn Avenue, where they were the first to defy the Mostyn Estate ruling that all leasehold property should be painted brown or green. They painted the exterior cream and when Lord Mostyn's agent called and told them to conform they challenged him to take them to court – a challenge that was not taken up. The Dorchester was converted into fifteen flats in 1989.

Beyond lies a delightful open area known as Bodafon Fields, preserving an open view of the sea from Bodafon farm, which was the home of Mostyn Estate agent John Williams during the planning of the town. Opposite the fields the children's paddling pool was the scene of a notorious murder in 1993. Howard Hughes, a 31-years-old former mental patient from Colwyn Bay, was convicted of the rape and murder of seven-years-old Sophie Hook, from Great Budworth, whose body was found on the shingle just below the pool. She had been abducted while sleeping with friends in a tent in the back garden of her uncle's home, in nearby Craigside. It was assumed she had been dragged across Bodafon Fields.

Since 1983 there have been several proposals for developing Bodafon fields. In 1982 the Wales Tourist Board commissioned a report on the future of Llandudno's historic tourist industry in the face of cheap foreign competition. Within months the Board joined Mostyn Estates in a feasibility study for an *Alice in Wonderland* theme park in the Happy Valley. A few months later the author was in the United States with Mostyn Estates' chief agent George Hiller, and his architect, on a Wales Tourist Board study tour of theme parks in Florida and Virginia. Somewhere in Disney World's 43 square miles (111sq km) Mr. Hiller turned to the author and said: "Perhaps the Happy Valley is not the right place for a Llandudno theme park. We might be able to come up with an alternative site." Upon his return to Llandudno Mr. Hiller soon produced a scheme for Bodafon fields, where the centrepiece would have been a Disney World-style castle based on the architecture of Penmorfa, the house that Alice's father built on Llandudno's West Shore in 1862. There would also have been substantial housing within the scheme. It attracted massive opposition and after a lengthy planning inquiry in 1987 the scheme was rejected, largely because of the traffic problems it might cause on existing roads. All subsequent schemes (all incorporating housing) have attracted matching opposition – including a plan that would link the development to a park-and-ride service using an electric tram that would trundle into town through the already congested streets and complex one-way system.

The eastern end of the promenade, which becomes known as Colwyn Road, was dominated from 1888 until 1974 by the Craigside Hydro Hotel, with a very prominent six-storey square tower. Princess Margaret, sister of Queen Elizabeth II, had an elegant three-course lunch there on 29 May 1951, while attending the 79th conference of the National Union of Teachers, at Llandudno. The Craigside Hydropathic Establishment was built by John Smith who, since 1876, had run a similar establishment at Limpley Stoke, near Bath. All the latter's main features were incorporated in his Llandudno building, which offered Turkish or Russian baths, spray baths, electric baths (i.e. a bath beneath a supposedly beneficial electric light) and massage given by either a man or woman, according to one's preference. There was also a resident physician, Dr. John Miles Chambers, brother-in-law of John Smith. Mrs. Smith died in 1901 and was buried at Limpley Stoke, according to her wish, and a year later John Smith retired to Weston-super-Mare, taking his family with him.

They included his granddaughter Violet Mary Firth, who was born on 6 December 1890 at Bryn-y-bia, a house that later became an outstanding country house hotel until demolished in January 2001, to be replaced by a block of flats, called Bryn-y-bia Lodge. It stood on the corner of Colwyn Road and Bryn-y-bia road. Violet Firth was to earn fame as Dion Fortune, who believed herself to be a priestess of the occult who could remember several of her incarnations dating from her time in Atlantis, the lost continent of legend. She died in January 1946 and for many years afterwards was a cult figure in the world of magic. Craigside Hydro was closed in 1974, followed by a three-day auction of its contents. The impressive building was demolished in 1975, to be replaced during 1979 by 21 houses, with a further 23 across the road on what had been the hotel's indoor tennis court, later converted into a rink for ice shows.

Villa Marina, on the opposite side of the road was built for a Midlands cake and biscuit millionaire named Scribbans, who died before it was completed. It was intended to look like a ship when viewed from the sea but ended up looking more like one of his cakes, and was dubbed Scribona Castle after one of his brand names. Birkenhead Corporation bought it for £15,200 in 1965, to provide seaside holidays for old and handicapped people. Wirral Council acquired it in the 1974 reorganisation of local government, and closed it in 1977. It is now a hotel.

Craigside Inn, a little higher up the hill, was originally a house known as Simdda (Simdde) Hir, its most famous resident being Hugh Mulleneux Walmsley, who described himself as a Colonel in the Imperial Ottoman Army. In 1864 he wrote *Llandudno as it is* (having earlier written books about soldiering in Algeria). Simdda Hir became St. Mary's Convent in 1969 but the nuns left in 1984, after which it was converted into the Craigside Manor Hotel, until sold to its present users.

Sydney Muschamp's delightful Llandudno beach scene, painted in 1878 (above), hung for many years at the County Hotel, in Craig-y-don, but is now in Sheffield.

Regular crossings of the River Conwy were made to and from Deganwy. Many of the passengers would have been staying in nearby Llandudno.

BEACH SCENE

An Englishman who toured North Wales in 1795 noted, with ingenuous surprise: "They have a strange custom here that has an air of great indelicacy to the stranger: which is that the inferior orders of people commonly bathe without the usual precautions of machines and dresses."

Bathing machines got to Llandudno in 1855 but another decade elapsed before the Improvement Commissioners introduced bylaws against nude bathing. A bathing machine was a horse-drawn changing room which the user would enter on dry land and leave, holding ten yards of safety line, only when it had been placed in sufficient depth of water "to prevent the bather or bathers therefrom indecently exposing his, her or their person or persons." When the user, at 6d. (2½p) for forty minutes, had swum enough he would re-enter the machine and wave a flag through a hole in the roof, as a signal to be hauled up the beach. The machines had to operate within two clearly defined areas, that from St. George's Hotel to Clonmel Street being the Ladies' Bathing Ground, after which 150 yards (137m) of forbidden territory led to the Gentlemen's Bathing Ground which commenced in the vicinity of what is now the Imperial Hotel and terminated at the eastern end of Mostyn Crescent.

Under the 1855 regulations the bathing machine proprietors had to supply "bathing-gowns for ladies," but there was no obligation upon women to wear them, and no form of bathing dress was stipulated for men. In 1864 the Commissioners asked their Inspector of Nuisances to report

The Llandudno panorama drawn in 1888, showing the Baths and Baths Hotel, and the new Pier Pavilion. The hydraulic lift tower has been added to St.George's Hotel.

upon alleged embarrassment caused to ladies staying in Mostyn and Neville Crescents – overlooking the Gentlemen's Bathing Ground. Commissioner Morris Pritchard said that in almost every instance the men bathed naked, and in such close proximity to the promenade and the hotels. John Williams, Clerk to the Commissioners, warned that if they kept driving the naked men ever further eastwards along the beach, as had already happened once, Llandudno would soon cease to be a bathing place. The Inspector of Nuisances said that although bathing machines had been equipped with aprons or drawers no man would wear such a garment after it had been used by someone else, hence the general custom of bathing nude.

In 1865 the Commissioners introduced new bathing by-laws making it an offence for a man to bathe without an apron or drawers. At the same time the Ladies Bathing Ground was extended from the St. George's Hotel to the Imperial, with a 200 yards (183m) zone separating it from the men. "Any gentleman who shall bathe within 200 yards (183m) of the Ladies' Bathing Ground, or any lady who shall bathe within 200 yards (183m) of the Gentlemen's Bathing Ground, shall forfeit a sum not exceeding forty shillings," said the new by-laws.

Great strides had been made by 1894 when, as one of their last acts before handing over to the new Urban Council of January 1895, the Commissioners resolved to allow mixed bathing. A special area of the beach was set aside, opposite the Arcadia, subject to families using the bathing machines and wearing "the University or full bathing costume," but Llandudno was torn asunder when Mrs Tamar Griffiths, of Osborne House, chanced to see a photograph of a girl in bathing costume on the town Publicity Committee's desk in 1935. In the ensuing row an official statement was issued denying that Llandudno had any intention of introducing "bathing belles" to their guidebook.

Bathing machines remained in use at Llandudno until 1958, when 80-years-old William Jones, of St. Beuno's Road, decided to retire, and sold them at £4/10s (£4.50) each, for use as garden sheds. He was the last of the bathing machine proprietors and was still using a horse to haul them in and out of the sea until 1946. His machines were a prominent feature of the filming, in 1951, of Arnold Bennett's *The Card*, starring Sir Alec Guinness, Glynis Johns, Valerie Hobson and Petula Clark. Miss Hobson was last seen at Llandudno in 1967 when she accompanied her husband, John Profumo, to the Conservative party conference at the Pier Pavilion.

While unable to do anything about the nude men on their beach in 1864 the Improvement Commissioners wasted no time in banning "Punch and Judy, his dog and all the noisy paraphernalia belonging thereto," in July of the same year. However, Richard Codman successfully appealed against his banishment and there has been a Professor Codman on Llandudno's waterfront ever since. This was Codman's first season. He was born in Norwich to a family of Hungarian Romany origin, and when he was 18 became a travelling entertainer, initially with a banjo and fiddle, and for a time as a bare-knuckle challenger working the fairs, in partnership with Jem Mace. Upon his marriage in 1859 he was given a caravan and two horses, with which he and his wife wandered the country, scratching a living as travelling Gypsies. When they turned up at Llandudno in 1864 one of the horses died, and with no money to buy a replacement Richard, then aged 33, found casual work and spent his spare time collecting drift wood off the beach, from which he carved a set of Punch & Judy characters. He obviously already knew the rudiments of the ancient art of Punchinello, which he believed began as a Middle Ages play about Pontius Pilate and Judas Iscariot, before turning up in England in the 17th century. There is a family tradition that Charles Dickens modelled his Thomas Codlin, of *The Old Curiosity Shop* (1841), on a Codman. His income was derived from employing a one-armed "bottler" who went among the crowd with a collecting box, carefully holding five flies, which Codman would place in his hand. Five flies at the end of the collection was Codman's proof that the one-armed man had not kept anything for himself!

While performing at Llandudno in the summer Codman would spend the winters on Liverpool's

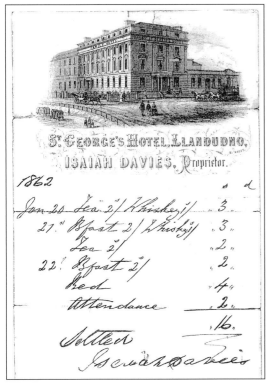

Bed and breakfast at St.George's Hotel cost 30p when the founder signed this bill in 1862.
The menu is adorned with the cipher of King Carol of Roumania for a dinner served to his
consort Queen Elisabeth at the Adelphi Hotel in 1890.
The busy 1920s beach scene below is at Penrhyn Bay, but the pier is industrial.

Contrasting beachwear at Llandudno: Edwardian, above; below, a bather in 1922.

Lime Street, and also found music hall engagements across Britain. He gave four command performances to Queen Victoria and the Prince and Princess of Wales, at Windsor and Sandringham, and to the Queen of Romania at Llandudno. He also performed privately for the local gentry, including the Duke of Westminster, the Marquess of Anglesey and Lord Mostyn. His son Herbert carried on the tradition at Llandudno for another 52 years and his son Richard II continued to perform in Liverpool, and both were followed by their children.

Llandudno has always been a good place for banning things; like the proposed Liverpool Liberal Federation conference of 1895. "If we allow this we could not very well refuse to allow Anarchists or Socialists," said Councillor Thomas Thomas Marks (the retired town engineer, of Plas Myrddin, Abbey Road, and father of J.J.Marks). Sunday boating was banned in 1896. Then there was the Rev. John Woods, summonsed and fined in 1898 for preaching on the beach. The vintage years were the 1930s, commencing with a Council edict in 1932 that the then popular song *Ain't it grand to be bloomin' well dead,* had to be deleted from Llandudno programmes. A circus was banned in 1933 because the council feared it would be unfair competition for other entertainments provided by ratepayers. Another decision of the same year presented policemen with the problem of deciding whether any music they heard on Sundays fell outside the privileged "classical" category – a dilemma of Jazz Banned! Also in 1933 came the Council ban on aircraft using the skies over Llandudno for advertising, this being the era of both skywriting and the towed slogan. Boxing was banned in 1934 as "unsuitable entertainment for Llandudno." The most recent noteworthy ban was in 1971, when an unnamed councillor removed a painting entitled *Adam and Eve* from an art exhibition at the town library. It had been painted by William Richardson who, in the holiday season, did portraits on Llandudno Pier.

One of the most popular features of Llandudno's beach, surviving from Victorian times, is the provision of donkey rides, from near the lifeboat slipway. Llandudno's boatmen are, alas, a dwindling race, which is a great pity because their trips around the cliffs and caves of the Great Orme form one of the finest maritime treats in Britain. The esteem in which these men are held may be gauged from the promenade memorial erected in 1965 in honour of Edward Jones, better known as Ted-yr-ogof, meaning "Ted of the cave," who died in 1965 on the slipway which he and his family had used for a century.

The Town Band has been a feature of the promenade since 1871. Since early in the last century they have had a fixed bandstand, near the Imperial Hotel, but between 1877 and 1910 they had a mobile platform, known as the Juggernaut, which used to be towed by horses to various vantage points. The first known band to parade on the promenade was a German band, in 1857. Before the advent of Ministry of Defence cut-backs in the 1990s famous military bands, notably the Royal Marines, Welsh Guards and Royal Welch Fusiliers, frequently beat the retreat on the promenade.

Though loved by many tourists, who mistakenly feed them, Llandudno's greedy and aggressive herring gulls are a pest. They will snatch food of any description from one's hand and will take jewellery or other interesting items visible through an open hotel window. They will rifle through waste paper bins, hauling out bags which they then tear open. Countless hundreds of the gulls have abandoned the Great and Little Orme cliffs to nest on urban roofs, from where they will attack anyone seen as a threat to their fledglings. From time to time there have been proposals to try to ban the feeding of the gulls but the bird lovers always win the day.

Llandudno pier's new entrance, photographed in 1904. The original pier entrance and 1884 extension are shown below – the steamer is La Marguerite, soon to leave to serve as a troopship for World War One.

THE PIER

8

Llandudno Pier is 2,295 feet (699m) long and the envy of every other Welsh resort, both as a superb piece of Victoriana and, until 1982, as a very practical terminal for the big ships of the Isle of Man Steam Packet Company. It is the town's second pier – and much altered at that. As noted in Chapter 2, the first was a useless ornament built in 1858 to protect the rights of the St. George's Harbour & Railway Company. That pier was demolished by the infamous storm of 25/26 October 1859 that resulted in the loss of 223 vessels and 800 lives on the shores of Britain. In North Wales it is remembered as the storm which cost 444 lives when the 719-ton steam clipper *Royal Charter* was wrecked at Moelfre, east Anglesey, near the end of a 16,000 mile (25,749km) voyage from Australia. She was carrying a cargo of gold bullion and most of her passengers were on their way home to Liverpool with personal fortunes from the Australian gold fields. Llandudno's first pier was patched up after the storm and used for disembarking passengers during high tides, until the present pier was built.

In 1875 the new Llandudno Pier Company obtained an Act to enable them to build the present structure. The first pile was driven on 10 July 1876 by Glasgow builders Walter Macfarlane and the straight section of the Pier, 1,200 ft (366m) long (from the gate near Happy Valley) was opened to the public on 1 August 1877, with ironwork cast at Elmbank Foundry, Glasgow. The spur, which now gives the Pier its main entrance from the promenade, was added in 1884, a new landing stage was built in 1891, reinforced in 1904, and replaced by the present steel and concrete pier head in 1969.

Early users of the present pier head were the Prince of Wales, followed an hour later by Princess Anne (now the Princess Royal), when the Royal Yacht *Britannia* anchored in the bay on 2 July 1969, escorted by HMS *Llandaff*. A year earlier Princess Alice, granddaughter of Queen Victoria, arrived incognito at the pier from the Norwegian cruise ship *Meteor* (she died in 1981). A galaxy of unannounced European royalty disembarked in May 1972 from the 5,813-ton German ship *Regina Maris*. They included Prince Moritz of Hesse and Rhine, accompanied by his wife, the former Princess Tatjana of Sayn-Wittgenstein-Berleburg. Also in the party was Princess Margaret of Hesse, daughter of Lord Geddes, who married into the Prussian royal family in 1937. There, too, was Princess Beatrix, 36-years-old daughter of Prince Gottfried of Hohenlohe-Langenburg and his wife the former Princess Margarita of Greece. Others who came tumbling out of the ship included the Comtesse d'Eudeville, of Paris, the Earl and Countess Waldegrave of Bath, Lord and Lady Strathcoma of Colonsay, and Lady Stainton of Canterbury. More familiar names included Sir Ronald Orr Ewing, Miss A.J.Boyd Carpenter and Admiral Sir Angus Cunninghame Graham. They were identified thanks to a foreign aristocrat who gave his passenger list to the author, whose passion for maritime history prompted him to walk down the pier for a closer look at the strange ship, just as the passengers disembarked.

Next day the 26,677-ton Swedish-American luxury liner *Kungsholm* anchored at Llandudno to disembark 400 passengers on a millionaires' outing from New York. These annual visits by the sister ships *Kungsholm* or *Gripsholm* were advertised in the United States as being "for Americans who have seen everywhere else." One such visit, on 6 May 1968, came within an ace of a major disaster, watched from the shore by thousands of people. The *Kungsholm* was anchored 1¹/₂ miles (2.5km) offshore, and using the 314-ton *St.Trillo* as a tender. Having collected 325 passengers from Llandudno pier the tender was about to tie up alongside the *Kungsholm* when a rope fouled her port propeller. Also on board the tender were several members of the *Kungsholm's* crew and about 50 local residents who had paid half-a-crown (25p) for a closer look at the visiting liner. As the *St.Trillo* drifted away the overworked starboard engine failed. She was within minutes of striking the Little Orme by the time Llandudno lifeboat arrived from another rescue, and was able to hold her off long enough for the Rhyl and Moelfre lifeboats, and the Conwy trawler *Kilravock* to join the rescue, and haul her back to the pier. Swedish American Line later got into financial difficulties and sold their two famous liners during October-December 1975. The *Kungsholm* was later renamed *Sea Princess* and is now the P&O liner *Victoria*.

The Royal Navy were regular users of the pier into the 1970s, both on courtesy visits and for cloak and dagger operations by the fishery protection patrols when French, Belgian and Dutch trawlers tried to snatch a crafty catch off the Great Orme in the days before Britain surrendered her fishing rights to the Brussels administration of the European Economic Community. On one day in May 1965 warships operating out of Llandudno boarded and arrested seven Belgian trawlers within the 12 mile (19km) limit – but another 43 got away. One warship that never got here was H.M.S. *Llandudno*, a 656-ton minesweeper completed in March 1942. After anti-submarine patrols in the Minches she was sent to Iceland in October 1942 and for the next twelve months carried out sweeping and patrol duties in that area, including two months in the Denmark Straits. In November 1943 the *Llandudno* returned to home waters for minesweeping duties off the east coast and in the English Channel, until paid off at Lowestoft in March 1945.

Perhaps the most famous (at least in the short term) of the many colourful sailors who have used Llandudno Pier was Seaman Richard Starkey, a £3.50 a week steward on the pleasure steamer *St.Tudno* during 1957. As Ringo Starr he returned to Llandudno in 1963, a member of a relatively unknown pop group called The Beatles, who gave six performances, during 12-17 August, at the Odeon, in Gloddaeth Street. They were back again in 1964 for a Sunday

Llandudno's proud musical tradition was born in the 1877 pier head bandstand.

The construction of the Pier Pavilion in 1886, and below, the opening of the colonnaded entrance to Happy Valley in April 1932.

evening concert. Four years later Ringo Star and his companions George Harrison, John Lennon and Paul McCartney were all made Members of the Most Excellent Order of the British Empire.

Probably the biggest number of ships using Llandudno Bay on any one day was on 25 June 1968. The *Patricia,* flagship of Trinity House, was here all day. HMS *Keppel*, a frigate, arrived at 9am, soon followed by the *King Orry*, belonging to the Isle of Man Steam Packet Company. Another Isle of Man ship, the *Snaefell*, came in the afternoon, followed by the Isles of Scilly Steamship Company's *Queen of the Isles*. The Isle of Man company's *Manxman* arrived in the evening, at the end of what used to be very popular day return trips between Llandudno and Douglas.

Llandudno's more conventional musical tradition dates from 1877 when Tyler's Band was engaged to play in a small hexagonal bandstand at the pier head. There were seven musicians, men and women, who wore a uniform of trousers, frock coats and pillbox hats. It was to this little bandstand that Jules Rivière, a former French army musician, was appointed in 1887 to conduct what had blossomed into the Pier Orchestra of 28 musicians. He first made the headlines when, as a youth in Paris, he was spotted wrestling with Jacques Offenbach on the pavement of the Champs Elysées, in a dispute over the services of a particular singer. His many "firsts" included a Welsh promenade concert at Covent Garden in 1873, using only Welsh music and musicians, backed by the first (and probably the last) bilingual Welsh/English posters outside the Royal Opera House. His soloists for that historic event included Brinley Richards (composer of *God Bless the Prince of Wales*) and John Thomas, better known as Pencerdd Gwalia, harpist to Queen Victoria.

To reach his new Llandudno bandstand he had to pass the enormous Pier Pavilion, opened in September 1886 (after some delays when the original ornate glass roof was blown off, to the great financial embarrassment of the Pier Company who promptly dismissed their engineer). The Pavilion was 204 ft (62m) long with a width ranging from 84 ft (26m) to 104 ft (32m), with canopy roof 60 ft (18m) across.

"There were differences of opinion at first between the directors and myself about using the Pavilion, they inclining to the belief that visitors would not, even for good music, consent to be shut indoors on fine summer evenings," recorded Rivière.

He won the day, went inside, and proceeded to treble the size of his orchestra, and began engaging soloists like Adelina Patti – whose sister Carlotta was an old friend from his Covent Garden days. Soon his reputation was nation-wide, and the young Henry Wood was sent to Llandudno to sit at the feet of the maestro and learn some of the showmanship he later put into the Proms. Sir Henry has left us his impressions of Rivière: "As I took my seat I saw an elderly gentleman seated in a gilded armchair, *facing the audience.* He was elegantly dressed in a velvet jacket on the lapel of which reposed a huge spray of orchids more fitted for a woman's corsage. He held a bejewelled ivory baton in his hand from which dangled a massive blue tassel. This he wound round his wrist. He bowed ceremoniously to the audience and tapped loudly on his golden music stand. Still seated (and still facing the audience), he began the Overture to *Mignon.*"

The Pier orchestra had dropped down to 34 musicians by 1925 when the company dispensed with conductor Arthur Payne, resulting in protest meetings and a very successful farewell fund. In 1926 he was replaced by 31-years-old Dr. Malcolm Sargent, who weeded out players unable to match his enthusiasm, introduced new blood and caused a torchlight procession of protest. He increased the orchestra to 42 musicians and stayed for two seasons. He was followed by John Bridge, who gave way to George Cathie in 1930. Two years later a young man named Paul Beard was whisked out of the Llandudno orchestra to become leader of Sir

Thomas Beecham's new London Orchestra. One of the Pier's guest conductors of that year was Sir Adrian Boult. He returned in 1933, as did Sir Walford Davies to play a piano concerto with the Pier orchestra.

Envious of the audiences Will Catlin's Follies were packing into the Arcadia, the Pier Company ended Llandudno's great days of resident symphony orchestras in 1936, and switched to variety. In 1938 John Morava took over the small variety orchestra, which he augmented on Sundays for some memorable evening concerts featuring leading solo vocalists, with whom he maintained the Pavilion's musical tradition until 1974, when the orchestra was disbanded.

Old posters adorning thin partition walls ripped out of a Pavilion basement store in 1969 perpetuated such names as Petula Clark, Bernard Miles, Eve Boswell, Rawicz & Landauer, Arthur Askey, Beverley Sisters, Semprini, Lucille Graham, Al Koran, George Formby, Ted Ray, Clarkson Rose, Cyril Fletcher, Robb Wilton, Geraldo, Vic Oliver and operatic soprano Anne Edwards.

As a popular centre for political rallies the Pavilion resounded to the voices of Lloyd George, Stanley Baldwin, Ramsay MacDonald, Oswald Mosley, Neville Chamberlain, Clement Attlee, Hugh Gaitskell, Winston Churchill, Anthony Eden, Harold Wilson, Harold Macmillan and Edward Heath. It was here that Baroness Margaret Thatcher began her political career when, as Margaret Roberts, she turned up for the 1948 Conservative Party conference as a member of the Oxford Graduates' Association. She was then a 23-years-old research chemist but during the course of the conference one of her Oxford friends suggested a political career and went on to recommend her to the Dartford delegates, who invited her to lunch at the Grand Hotel. She stood (unsuccessfully) for Dartford at the 1951 General Election, during the course of which she met Dennis Thatcher. She was back at Llandudno for the 1956 Party conference, and she eventually entered Parliament in 1959 as the Member for Finchley. She revisited Llandudno in 1978.

The British Union of Fascists was also seeded at Llandudno Pier Pavilion. Former Conservative MP Sir Oswald Mosley joined the Labour Party in 1924, and resigned as Chancellor of the Duchy of Lancaster in 1930 when Ramsay MacDonald's cabinet rejected his plan for economic recovery. After a twenty-minute speech to the 1930 Labour conference at Llandudno Mosley was acclaimed as a future Prime Minister, and within hours was re-elected to the National Executive from which he had been sent packing a year earlier. However the conference narrowly defeated a motion that would have established, as Party policy, the plan MacDonald had already rejected. Mosley saw it as a personal defeat and left Llandudno in a huff, to create his own black-shirted Fascist party.

Llandudno Pier Pavilion had another claim to fame as the scene of Llandudno's biggest banquet, in 1929, when 1,001 delegates of the National Union of Meat Traders sat down to a meal prepared by local caterer John E. Payne who was also the then chairman of the Urban Council.

Pantomime was introduced to the Pavilion for the first time in 1972 by local impresario and comedian Alex Munro, father of actress Janet Munro who had died in tragic circumstances a few days before she was due to travel to Llandudno for rehearsals in the family show.

Llandudno Pier was the last target of the Suffragettes in their campaign to secure votes for women. They unsuccessfully tried to set it on fire on the eve of World War One – the greater conflict causing them to declare a truce in their unlawful activities.

Today the site of the Pier Pavilion is just an ugly scar, for the building was destroyed by fire on the evening of Sunday, 13 February 1994. It had been derelict for several years and had been colonised by nests of squatters who had taken to tearing out any available timber with which to light fires to keep themselves warm.

Pier Pavilion orchestra on stage in 1910. Below is the Happy Valley open-air theatre in 1920.

Llandudno's North Parade, around the entrance to the Pier, was redesigned in 2000, as part of a scheme for raising the sea defences after the severe flooding of 10 June 1993 – which was not caused by the sea but by the inability of the drains to cope with $5^1/_2$ inches of rain in three hours, during high tide. The new pumping station that had opened on the West Shore about a year earlier failed, due to flooding of its electrical equipment. Llandudno's first sea wall, 100 yards (91m) long, was built in 1855 in front of North Parade. Three of the North Parade houses, built in 1852, look much the same as they are depicted in a watercolour of the same year by R. Green, father of R.Green of The Stowe, Church Walks. The painting shows Bay Court (originally Moranedd), where bay windows have been added to what was the first modern house on the seafront; View Villa (with extensive alterations); and Osborne House. We have already noted that Min-y-don, at the top of the hill, occupies the site of a water mill. The painting also shows a house (Tŷ John Jeffreys) that was demolished to make way for the corner of what is now Prince Edward Square.

Osborne House was still being built when Green painted the scene, for he has conjectured how it might look, when viewed from the rocks above the present Grand Hotel. Its origins are

The Gorsedd of Bards still carry the banner first used (above) at the Happy Valley in 1896, when Hwfa Môn, wearing the mitre, was the Archdruid.

wrapped in mystery, for it is still the only dressed stone house on the promenade, and was obviously designed to be a high quality residence for a gentleman of some stature. It was presumably named after the original Osborne House, rebuilt on the Isle of Wight in 1851, to the design of Prince Albert. Llandudno's Osborne House quickly became a boarding school, an extraordinary venture for this small isolated community of that period. It was run by two ladies known to history only as the Misses Williams – they were away from home on census night 1861, when the two pupil boarders were named as Frederick and Joseph Platt, aged 11 and 9, sons of John Platt, of the famous Oldham textile machinery company, and a director of the London & North Western Railway Company, who had a home at Llanfairfechan.

In 1883 it reverted to a gentleman's residence when John Walker (brother of Sir Andrew Walker of Liverpool art gallery fame) leased it from Lord Mostyn. Contrary to common belief he had no links with "Johnny Walker's Whisky," but lived on inherited profits from the famous Walker brewing family, whose name survived in Tetley Walker beers until 1999. When John Walker died in 1913 Osborne House was placed in trust for his wife to live there for life, after which it would pass to his son John Arthur Walker – who was a 24-years-old lieutenant in the 10th Battalion Royal Welch Fusiliers when killed at Ypres in 1916, and for whom there is a three-light memorial window in St. George's Church. Osborne House was remodelled inside to open as a six-suite luxury hotel in 2001.

Historically, perhaps the most interesting house in this section is the St. Tudno Hotel, at 15 North Parade, where it blocks off the ancient road from the beach to the old village. It was built by Thomas Jones, of Dwygyfylchi, who, with the aid of his English wife Eliza, opened it as the Tudno Villa Lodging House. Early in 1861 Thomas Jones received a letter asking for rooms for twelve for the Easter holiday, and in due course they all turned up: Dean Henry G. Liddell, of Christ Church, Oxford, his wife, five children, footman, lady's maid, nurse, Swiss nursery maid, and 28-years-old governess Mary Prickett. This was the first of many resident holidays in Llandudno for Alice Liddell, then aged eight and soon to be immortalised as the heroine of Lewis Carroll's *Alice's Adventures in Wonderland*. The family returned to Llandudno in the summer but on that occasion they stayed at the St. George's Hotel. By the following summer they owned their own house on the West Shore.

Tudno Villa was built to block off the original road from the promenade into town, known as Wynne Street. It continued across what is now 145 Mostyn Street, from where there was a junction eastwards into Mostyn Street, while the continuation went across part of the land on which the present Tabernacl church is built (the original building being beside Wynne Street).

During the remodelling of North Parade in 2000 the once famous weeping elms were felled by the contractors in February, a few days after the work started. They had been a highly attractive feature incorporated in millions of postcards for very many decades. The Council said they were not felled to help with the remodelling but because they had been infected with Dutch Elm Disease, unknown to people living in the area.

Belmont, at the junction of North Parade and Church Walks, conceals an old railway tunnel out of the Great Orme copper mines. Next-door-but-one, at No. 23 (now an annexe of the Knowsley Hotel at 24), we have what used to be Tŷ Gwyn, built out of copper profits to replace the original farm of the same name. In 1764 John Pierce, of Tŷ Gwyn, and Richard Powell, of Penmynydd (near the Half-Way Station on the Great Orme) were the only residents who owned Bibles, and probably the only two who could read. On the opposite side of the road stood the old Bijou Theatre.

Llandudno's first public conveniences, built in 1893, are a little higher up the road, against a cliff that used to be known as Clawdd-y-gored (meaning "weir-wall") in the days before the houses came to this corner of the Great Orme. Two years later town engineer E.P. Stephenson

THE LIVERPOOL AND NORTH WALES STEAMSHIP COMPANY LIMITED

RESUMPTION OF SAILINGS
EASTER · 1946
APRIL 19th to 22nd

DAILY SAILINGS
FROM PRINCES LANDING STAGE (Weather and other circumstances permitting)
SUBJECT TO ALTERATION WITHOUT NOTICE AND TO CONDITIONS OF CARRIAGE

"ST. SEIRIOL"
WILL SAIL

Good Friday, Saturday, Easter Sunday and Monday

Leaving		Each Day	*Leaving*		Each Day
LIVERPOOL	... ...	10 45 a.m.	MENAI BRIDGE	...	3 45 p.m.
LLANDUDNO	{ arr.	1 5 p.m.	LLANDUDNO	{ arr.	5 5 ,,
	{ dep.	1 15 ,,		{ dep.	5 15 ,,
MENAI BRIDGE	arr.	2 35 ,,	LIVERPOOL	... arr.	7 30 ,,

N.B.—Bangor and Beaumaris passengers with single or period tickets proceed from Menai Bridge, P.O. Square (free Bus conveyance).

DAILY SAILINGS will recommence SATURDAY, MAY 18th
For Particulars and Fares, see later Bills.

Llandudno

HOLIDAY GUIDE (9d postage) FROM R.P. MOORE TOWN HALL LLANDUDNO [BRITISH RAILWAYS]

A poster for the post-war resumption of steamship sailings from Liverpool to Llandudno. Newly nationalised British Railways also issued posters for renewed excursions to Llandudno. The St.Seiriol is seen at the pier head in the photograph by Dave Williams taken from one of the new cable cars in 1969.

found himself still having to defend the provision of public conveniences, telling the Incorporated Association of Municipal Engineers he hoped the prejudice "which has been so markedly shown will in time die away, and that it will be seen, as in other towns, that such conveniences are not only a necessity but an advantage to the town." According to tradition, unsupported by any written evidence, the lavatory building or adjacent wall seals off an old cave which used to lead into the mines, and which the Baths Hotel adapted for use as a wine cellar. Today's visitors to Llandudno might be excused for thinking there is still a prejudice against the provision of public conveniences. The name Clawdd-y-gored reminds us of the ancient Llandudno fish-trap in which it is claimed that as many as 10,000 herrings were left stranded on one turn of the tide in 1847.

The Grand Hotel, with 156 bedrooms, is the biggest hotel in North Wales and was the biggest in Wales until the fairly recent developments in Cardiff. It was built for Francis Doyle with stone quarried from Ffolt, behind the old village of Glanwydden. It opened in 1901 on the site of the Baths, Reading Room & Billiard Hall built in 1855, and the western annexe that became the Baths Hotel in 1879. When demolished in 1900 the Baths Hotel provided the rubble to fill up what was then Britain's biggest indoor swimming pool, opened in 1884 beneath the Pier Pavilion. Replenished by the sea on each tide, the Pavilion swimming pool was 160 ft (49m) long and 48 ft (15m) wide.

The most famous patron of the Baths was our famous but incoherent adversary of the Crimean War, General the Prince Mikhail Dimitrievich Gorchakov, defender of Sevastopol. He and the Grand Duke Mikhail, brother of Tsar Alexander II, spent a holiday at Llandudno in 1858 when the general's principal pastime was challenging other users of the Baths to a game of chess, although his eyesight was said to be very poor. Midway through their stay they were joined by the Crown Prince of Wurtemberg.

The register at the Grand Hotel used to read like an edition of *Who Was Who*. A little story worth recording relates to Sir Winston Churchill's last visit, in the autumn of 1948, when the Conservative Party was in conference at the Pier Pavilion. Soon after Sir Winston had been installed in Room 109 he confounded the management by asking for a candle. It was a Friday evening, the shops were shut, and it was only with some difficulty that the hotel obtained both a supply of candles and a candlestick worthy of so important a visitor. Not until the next day did the reason for the strange request become apparent – Sir Winston used a candle to light his cigars.

Another anecdote relating to the Grand concerns the night in 1965 when the manager, World War Two pilot Max Aiken, decided to substitute Welsh for the then traditional French on the restaurant menu. He saw it as a great patriotic and logical gesture and the Press were on hand for its novel inauguration. "If we must feed our guests in a language they do not understand it is nonsense to perpetuate French when we have a home-cooked alternative that is at least relevant to their holiday experience," he said. His first diners were French, the waiter was Spanish, and their lingua franca was Pidgin English!

On 5 December 1973 an Irish arsonist caused £200,000 worth of fire damage to the Grand Hotel. He lit a second fire in room 414 sixteen days later, but was then arrested and subsequently sentenced to life imprisonment.

Opposite the Grand a collonaded walk, opened in 1932, leads into the Happy Valley which was once a quarry still being worked until 1887, although it was an area which tourists discovered at least as long ago as 1860, when 18-years-old Lot Williams built a camera obscura on the mound still known as Camera Hill. The camera obscura was a darkened room, with a circular white table that acted as a screen for views picked up by lenses in a turret on the roof. It was always operated by descendants of Lot Williams until the last, David Jones, decided to close it in 1964, because of changing patterns of tourists' interests. The 4 ft (1.2m) screen ended up in the backyard of his home, at Madoc Terrace, Gyffin, but he left the lenses in place. The building was burnt down by vandals two years later. A replacement camera obscura has since been built on the hill.

Happy Valley Theatre was built in 1933 to replace an earlier structure destroyed by fire. A husband and wife team of "nigger minstrels" was providing open-air entertainment in this natural topographical theatre in 1873, using a bell-tent as their dressing room. Mr. Round's Promenade Band had played there a year earlier but it is with the minstrel tradition that we associate the open-air theatre. The building was destroyed by an arsonist in 1987 and never rebuilt. Exactly a century earlier Lord Mostyn closed the troublesome Happy Valley quarry and gave the area to the town as a permanent park, in commemoration of the fiftieth jubilee of Queen Victoria. Deep cart ruts were filled and grassed, trees and shrubs were planted, and this first phase of development was completed in August 1890 with the unveiling of the elegant drinking fountain, inscribed: "This fountain was erected in the Happy Valley to commemorate the Jubilee of the reign of Her Most Gracious Queen Victoria and Empress of India, by the Right Honourable Lady Augusta Mostyn, upon land presented to the town of Llandudno by her son, the Right Honourable Llewelyn 3rd Baron Mostyn. E.Jones, JP, Chairman, T.T.Marks, CE, Clerk and Engineer, Llandudno Improvement Commissioners. 1887 ANNUS JUBILÆUS." The sculptor of the queen's bust was H.Montford. One side of the fountain displays the arms of Lord Mostyn and the opposite side the lozenge of Lady Augusta. Those commissioning the inscriptions were somewhat over obsequious in their erroneous use of the title "Right Honourable."

Large boulders (weighing up to 6 tons each) on the greensward were placed in position in 1962, for the Gorsedd ceremonies in conjunction with the 1963 National Eisteddfod. Stones used for a similar ceremony on the same site in 1896 were later incorporated in the rock gardens at the rear. These gardens contain numerous botanical curios including the Great Orme Cotoneaster *(Cotoneaster Vulgaris)*, first discovered in 1783, and which does not grow naturally anywhere else. The *Chrysanthemum Rubellum* originated here. It was discovered in 1929 and now grows successfully in many parts of the world.

The Great Orme Cabinlift, which has its bottom terminal in the Happy Valley, was opened on 30 June 1969 as the longest passenger cable car system in Britain. It was initially refused planning permission in 1967, and the promoter's appeal was supported by a majority of only two within Llandudno Urban Council. The distance to the Summit station is 1 mile 40 feet (1612m), and the four-seater cabins travel at 6½ mph (4.8 kmph) on an endless steel rope weighing 17 tons. The longest span between intermediate trestles is 1,023 feet (312m) and the maximum height at which the cabins travel in relation to the ground below is 160 feet (49m) – above the former Happy Valley quarry. It offers some spectacular vistas, which was just as well when teething troubles brought the system to a standstill for 90 minutes, with 34 passengers airborne, in August 1970, and for four hours, with 52 people in the cabins, in May 1971.

The body of Eirlys Roberts, a woman in her early thirties, from Colwyn Bay, was found in the Happy Valley in 1979. She had been strangled by 62-years-old Anglesey-born Arthur Phillip Wynne within weeks of his release from a life sentence for murdering a Bangor woman in 1967.

In 1985 Aberconwy Council (who had inherited Happy Valley from Llandudno Urban Council) agreed to the conversion of the miniature golf course, below Wyddfyd Cottage, into a 306 yards (280m) artificial ski slope, to be developed by a group of North Wales businessmen. The ski slope opened in 1987 and two years later the theatre site was converted into a car park.

North Parade in 1861, when the roads were surfaced only with loose limestone chippings, which raised clouds of dust when dry (above). The Grand Hotel replaced the Baths Hotel beside the Pier Pavilion (right).

Coach drivers used to describe the Marine Drive feature as the Great Orme nose. The drive replaced a hazardous footpath (Left & Below).

The Great Orme is encircled by Marine Drive, a shelf cut out of the sheer cliffs, and four miles (6km) long between tollgates. It begins below Happy Valley, beside a car park created in 1931 when Llandudno scrapped an interesting relic of World War One – a Tank Mark IV which, as *F22*, formed part of F Battalion (later the 6th Regiment) of the Royal Tank Corps, at the historic 1917 Battle of Cambrai. Consuming a gallon (4.5 litres) of petrol for every mile (1.6km) to travel at its top speed of $3^1/2$ mph (5.6kmph), the 27 ton monster was driven out of Llandudno Station in 1922, by Lieut. Kim Farrar who had commanded it at Cambrai. In Chapel Street he relinquished his command to a local hero, Clement Arnold, who won the DSO as a 24-years-old lieutenant with the same tank battalion at the Battle of Amiens, in August 1918. Mr. Arnold drove *F22* to its final resting place, overlooking the Pier. Nine years later the Urban Council offered the tank for £1 to anyone who would take it away. There were no offers and the Council paid a Manchester scrap metal firm to demolish it – a task that took eight days.

Marine Drive was preceded by Cust's Path, a hazardous footway made between 1856-58 on the instructions of Reginald Cust, a London barrister and trustee of Mostyn Estate, who was knighted in 1890 as an authority on land administration in India. He charged a penny toll for the up-keep of the path but in 1868 Prime Minister William Gladstone, on a visit to Dean Liddell, complained it was so dangerous he had to be blindfolded and led along some particularly difficult sections by the Dean and his family, including Alice, of *Wonderland* fame. In April 1869 the town Commissioners ordered £10 of ratepayers' money to be spent on the provision of railings at the worst parts.

In 1872 the Great Ormes Head Marine Drive Co. Ltd. issued their prospectus for a £14,000 conversion of Cust's Path into the present roadway. Their chairman was St. John Charlton, of Holywell (who, in 1881, married Elizabeth Hughes, of Kinmel, a cousin of Alice Liddell) and the advertised engineers were Hedworth Lee, of the London & North Western Railway, at Bangor, and George Felton, the Mostyn Estate surveyor since 1857. The other directors were George Walker, of Gloddaeth and Manchester; Joseph Evans, of Haydock Grange, St.Helens; George Fielding, of Llandudno and the Manchester Stamp Office Buildings; Dr. James Nicol, Llandudno; Major T. Legh Thursby, of Queen's Gate, London; James Cutts, Llandudno; Thomas Williams, chemist, of Llandudno; Thomas Henry Lloyd, Llandudno; and Thomas Jones, Llandudno. In addition to cutting the road around the Orme the company intended "laying out gardens on the line of the road of the kind usually met with at the most favourable watering places, and to build a pavilion or music hall, conservatories, and marine aquaria, and generally provide further attractions for visitors to the town of Llandudno." Parliament approved the scheme in 1873, but people were slow to subscribe the £20 shares and it was September 1875 before the first sod was cut. The company went bankrupt and a second company completed the road.

A plaque on the tollgate, recording the completion of the road in 1878, names the engineer as Abraham Foulkes, of Ruabon, although he had only just arrived at Llandudno as the new agent and architect of Mostyn Estates (following the death of Felton), building Roden Villa, at 23 Trinity Square, as his home. Foulkes married a daughter of Jeremiah Bradley, a mining engineer who had an interest in Ruabon red clay and other minerals. A sister of Mrs. Foulkes married Jenkin Humphreys, who was the father of Foulkes's successor as Mostyn agent, George Alfred Humphreys – who had been apprenticed to Foulkes. The Urban Council bought Marine Drive for £10,500 in 1897, and they abolished the pedestrian toll in 1930 – but retained what has since grown into a hefty motorcar toll, collected by Conwy County Borough Council, much to the dismay of residents who can no longer afford to take this very pleasant ride.

The first foot race around the Orme was held in February 1885, being won by E. R. Daines in 33 minutes 46^1/$_2$ seconds. Half-a-mile (0.8km) beyond the tollgate the traveller loses sight of the town as he proceeds around Pen-trwyn headland. Until the mid 1990s this was the location for a robust Coastguard lookout station, designed to watch the shipping lane from the Mersey pilot station at Point Lynas to Liverpool. As shipping declined and became safer, so the inshore activities in the bay, such as water-skiing and windsurfing, increased and became more hazardous – but were out of sight of the lookout. The lookout (and its partner on the West Shore) were demolished and replaced by a mobile patrol. In addition to watching the progress of passing shipping the Coastguards were responsible for Government coast rescue equipment, including breeches buoy rocket apparatus, which had been a feature of Llandudno since 1815 as testimony of the number of shipwrecks which occurred here in the days of sail. It was last used by the Llandudno team on 5 November 1967, when the 1,000-ton *Rethi Müller* was blown aground while moored at Penmaenmawr quarry pier. The equipment was set up to haul ashore what was thought to be the German captain's wife – but who was instantly recognized as a Llandudno woman who had spent the night on board! By 1990 all breeches buoy equipment had been withdrawn from the British coast, in recognition of the way in which military helicopters could do the job better and quicker. Llandudno Coastguards maintain a cliff rescue team, but the Llandudno Mountain Rescue Team founded in 1958 was disbanded in the 1980s.

Pigeons' Cave, on the shore beneath the site of the Coastguard station, has been the scene of numerous climbing accidents. It was also the location of some valuable Late Bronze Age relics now housed at the National Museum of Wales, and which were found by two schoolboys in 1898. Seemingly the brothers Lewis and Arthur Riddell were rummaging in debris behind a large loose rock when they found two gold ear-rings of a Celtic type familiar to archaeologists, a bronze palstave (axe-head designed for fitting into a handle instead of being socketed), and a finely-made socketed bronze point weighing only one ounce (28g) and presumed to have been an awl for leather work.

The cave forms part of a shallow bay known as Porth yr Helyg (meaning Harbour of the Willow Trees) where much of the stone for Conwy suspension bridge and its approach embankment was loaded into flats for the short sea journey around the Orme. Beyond the bay a narrow ledge of rock, stretching for a considerable distance along the water's edge, is known as Mainc-y-stiwardiaid (Bench of the Stewards). According to tradition, agents of Mostyn Estate who offend against the tenants are sentenced to spend one or more tides naked on this ledge. Alas the wish appears to have been father to the thought and there is no record of any agent ever having suffered such indignity!

Proceeding along Marine Drive one arrives at a Y-junction, with a zigzag road on the left leading to St. Tudno's church, where parts of the north wall date back to the 12th or 13th century. The other walls are mostly 15th century. Although the roof was blown off in 1839 the main timbers survived and were retained when the church was restored in 1855 (the walls then being pierced to make several new windows). During further restoration in 1906 debris was removed to reveal the original floor level. A piece of chestnut found among the debris was presumed to have fallen from the roof. It was fashioned into souvenir mallets, one of which is

Great Orme Lighthouse photographed in 1879, and still looking the
same although now a private house.

preserved at Llandudno Rectory. Open-air services are a popular Sunday morning feature during the summer – conducted from a stone pulpit built in the churchyard in 1914. It will be noted that local limestone was the most popular material for tombstones until the beginning of the 19th century when Conwy Valley and Merioneth slate took over (retaining their inscriptions with the clarity of the day they were carved).

The road past St. Tudno's church eventually joins the main road to the summit but, for our purposes, we shall retrace our steps down the zigzag (past the old curate's glebe farm of Dolfechan, now misnamed Old Rectory) to rejoin Marine Drive. A journey of nearly a mile (1.6km) brings one to the fortress-like former lighthouse built by the Mersey Docks & Harbour Board, to the design of George Fosbery Lyster, their chief engineer. It was taken over by Trinity House on 2 April 1873. Throughout its life the lighthouse used the original lantern, from which the light first shone on 1 December 1862 – several months before the completion of the building. The light, which stood 325 feet (99m) above high water spring tides, showed white from 099° to 243°, and then red to 251°, being obscured elsewhere. Paraffin wick lamps were used in the lantern until 1904, vaporised petroleum mantle burners to 1923, and dissolved acetylene mantle lamp until 8 June 1965, from when it was electrified with 190,000-candle power. Relics preserved in the lighthouse included the original electric telegraph room, on a floor above the lantern. It remained intact until 1985, with all the equipment, disused since 1924, which in 1861 replaced the old semaphore link from Holyhead to Liverpool.

There was a full set of maritime signalling flags, several telescopes, an early Morse code key, and a paper-tape receiver, still containing paper. An 1846 weight-driven clock, removed from the summit semaphore station, adorned one of the walls, with an inscription reminding us that this was Station No. 5. It kept time until Trinity House switched off the light on 22 March 1985. The 1862 logbook was still stored in a desk in the central hall which divided the building into two houses, originally intended for the keeper and his deputy. The book showed that Job Jones, formerly of the semaphore station on the summit, was both lighthouse keeper and keeper of the electric telegraph on 31 January 1863. The overhead electric telegraph lines from the lighthouse used to go over the Orme and down Monks' Path, on the West Shore, to link up with Conwy. The lantern was taken to Liverpool where it stood in the foyer of the Mersey Docks and Harbour administration until 1993, when it was returned to Llandudno for display in the visitor centre at the summit of the Great Orme. The old lighthouse had been a private house for sixteen years when it was put on the market in 2001 for £825,000.

Derelict structures that could be seen on the skyline above the lighthouse until December 1975, and traces of which may still be discerned, were observation posts, built in September 1940 when the Royal Artillery Coast Artillery School was evacuated from its traditional home at Shoeburyness, Essex, to massive new gun emplacements on the southwestern shelf of the Great Orme and the eastern shoulder of the Little Orme. At its peak, in 1942, the Llandudno artillery school accommodated 150 officers, 115 officer cadets and 445 other ranks. Fourteen courses could be run simultaneously, and in addition to the gunnery wing, with its target ships anchored at sea, there were wireless and searchlight wings, and an officer cadet unit added in 1941. Its bigger buildings were removed in the 1950s.

Ruinous (and extremely dangerous) steps from this point, above the old lighthouse, lead down the cliffs to a man-made grotto, called the Llech or Hiding Cave, some 30 feet (9m) above the sea, and known to be over 400 years old. It has been constructed within a natural fissure, so that it is difficult to locate from the sea. It is hexagonal, about 7 ft (2m) in diameter and 8 ft (2.4m) high, made of squared blocks of limestone. There is a continuous stone bench around the interior wall and in the centre there is a stone pedestal that held a round stone table, now overthrown. The grotto contains a stone basin, fed by spring water, which overflows into an artificial bath excavated in the rock below, but now obscured by rock-fall. Its purpose remains a mystery apart from a poem entitled *Cywydd i'r Llech yn Llandudno* written by Siôn Dafydd Las, poet to the Nannau family at Dolgellau, who died in 1694. He described what we see today with considerable accuracy but added: "In a cave beneath the work a kitchen and wine-cellar lie," suggesting that much of the structure is now buried. He said it was "repaired with skill and taste for Mostyn's Heir, a man of wit," an apparent reference to William Mostyn who became MP for Flintshire in 1553. The cave was visited by Charles Darwin in 1824.

It was off here, on the night of 13 August 1915, that two German submarines, the *U-27* and *U-38* kept a rendezvous designed to rescue three officers who had escaped from a prisoner-of-war camp at Dyffryn Aled, Llansannan. They had received instructions in coded letters, following an initial contact via a repatriated civilian who had been interned as an enemy alien, and who was repatriated in a Christmas exchange. The escape plot was described to the author in 1960 by Otto Neuerberg, of Kiel, who accompanied his commanding officer, Kapitänleutnant Heinrich von Hennig, into captivity after their *U-18* was sunk. "Already at the camp when we arrived were Korvettenkapitän Hermann Tholens, formerly of the cruiser *Mainz*, and Gardes du Korps Rittmeister [cavalry captain] Wolf-Dietrich Baron von Helldorf – cousin of the notorious Wolf Heinrich Graf von Helldorf who became head of the *Sturm Abteilungen* (Storm Troopers) in Nazi Berlin-Brandenburg, but who was later involved in the unsuccessful July 1944 plot to overthrow Hitler, for which he was executed."

The *U-38* kept up the vigil for three nights, as planned, and then sailed away believing the officers had failed to get out of the camp. With the *U-38* on station her commander, Korvettenkapitän Max Valentiner, released the *U-27* which sailed away – to change the pattern of submarine warfare for ever more.

The escaped prisoners, who walked back into town at the end of the three days, discovered after the war that they were in the next cove to the one in which they were being sought, the *U-38* having come in much closer than they anticipated! Shortly before 9am, on 16 August, Korvettenkapitän Tholens entered the barber and tobacconist's shop of W.S.Herbert at 26 Mostyn Street, and asked for a packet of Abdullah cigarettes. There was by then a general alert throughout the area, and failing to recognise the stranger Herbert spoke in Welsh to another customer and asked him to follow the man until he met up with a soldier or a policeman. Strolling up the road Tholens next called at the Cocoa House, 66 Mostyn Street (now Johnson's shop), and ordered a coffee and a cake. Police Constable Morris Williams was alerted and kept observation from across the road, then followed him into the Tudno Hotel (now The Plumes), at No.64, where he challenged and arrested him. Tholens spent the night the old Police Station, in Court Street.

His two companions were more fortunate. They remained at liberty until 11pm when they were spotted near the Pier gates by cabman Alfred Davies, whose suspicions were immediately aroused. "Cab, Sir?" he asked, and after Baron von Helldorf and Kapitänleutnant von Hennig took their seats, and asked for the railway station, he drove them the short distance to Bryn Elli, in Gloddaeth Street, then serving as headquarters of the 15th (1st London Welsh) Battalion, Royal Welch Fusiliers, where he hailed the sentry. Davies's cab was used to take the prisoners first to the Imperial Hotel, where they appeared before the 113 Brigade Major, and from thence to the Royal Hotel, still in civilian use in Church Walks. Unlike Tholens, who was languishing in an old police cell, the other two had come under military jurisdiction, and were given food and a night of luxury thought appropriate for officers. The *U-38* survived the war and surrendered to the French, when the log book confirmed the Llandudno escapade.

The *U-27* had sunk 22 steamers, five trawlers and three sailing ships on her way to the Llandudno rendezvous. Six days after leaving Llandudno she challenged and stopped the freighter *Nicosian*, which was carrying a cargo of mules from New Orleans. Responding to a signal "Captured by submarine," the then still secret British Q-ship *Baralong* was soon on the scene. Q-ships were ingeniously armed merchant ships disguised to retain an innocent appearance but manned by Royal Navy volunteers in civilian clothes. Korvettenkapitän Bernd Wegener, on the conning tower of the *U-27*, ignored the *Baralong* as he commenced to shell the *Nicosian*, from which the crew had been allowed to take to the lifeboats. Rapidly closing the distance Lieut-Commander Godfrey Herbert, aboard the *Baralong*, hoisted the White Ensign, dropped the false sides and fired 34 shells, which sank the U-boat in less than two minutes. About twelve of the submariners managed to swim to the *Nicosian* before her own crew could re-board her, and when it became apparent that the Germans were trying to get away with their prize Herbert drew alongside to put a party of Royal Marines on board.

The next few minutes were probably the most shameful in the history of the Corps, for as each unarmed German surrendered he was bayoneted or shot. There were no German survivors to tell of the atrocity but when the crew of the *Nicosian* returned to America they gave lurid accounts, which received worldwide publicity. The international outcry was such that Herbert was replaced – and blamed for setting the scene that enabled the Germans to execute Nurse Edith Cavell on 12 October. Thereafter U-boat commanders took to sinking small coasters on sight instead of first allowing the crews to take to the lifeboats.

Otto Neurberg told the author how the 1915 participants spent World War Two. Valentiner lived with him at Kiel; von Helldorf, who had been his regular bridge partner, volunteered for administrative service at Naval HQ; and Tholens was appointed Obergeneralarbeitsführer (labour leader) at Stuttgart.

Continuing along Marine Drive, a concrete road on the left is another 1940 relic – which was used for the first (and only) hovercraft ascent of the Orme on 28 October 1967, when Geoffrey Harding, of Wallasey, took it all the way to the summit. The road links up with some interesting footpaths into the heart of the Great Orme. Here the peregrine falcon was a familiar sight until World War Two when it was subjected to an extermination campaign, at the instigation of pigeon fanciers who persuaded the Government it was a serious threat to communications – its favourite food being carrier pigeons. The last recorded occasion when a peregrine was captured alive on the Orme was in July 1923. It was taken from a nest near the lighthouse and was being offered for sale at 35s (£1.75) outside the Market Hall, but the vendor was prosecuted by the Royal Society for the Protection of Birds and fined 5s (25p).

Another interesting element of the Great Orme wildlife is the large but elusive herd of white Kashmir goats, huge creatures with magnificent horns. They roam around the interior and frequently cross the Marine Drive in search of new pasture, yet there are residents who have lived in Llandudno all their lives without ever seeing them. These goats are descendants of a pair which the Shah of Persia gave to Queen Victoria soon after her Coronation, and which grew into the Windsor royal herd from which the Royal Welch Fusiliers (23rd Foot) have received their regimental goats since 1844. As commanding officer of the 2nd Battalion RWF during 1869-80, and of the Regimental Depot at Wrexham, 1880-85, Major-General Sir Savage Mostyn came into possession of a pair of Royal goats, which after breeding at Gloddaeth, were turned loose on the Orme towards the end of the nineteenth century. During World War One an attempt was made to capture some of these goats to provide mascots for four battalions of the RWF which were being raised in Llandudno, but the hunt was abandoned when half the herd jumped to their deaths over the cliffs. In 1990 a goat bred from one of the Great Orme herd joined the 1st Battalion RWF and became an interesting feature of parades through Berlin, which remained under Allied Military Government from 1945 until 1994. This was not the only Llandudno goat to serve abroad with the Army. In the Royal Welch Fusiliers Regimental Museum, at Caernarfon Castle, there is a horned goat's skull with a brass plate stating it began its working life hauling a baby cart in Llandudno but joined the Army, and sailed for India with the RWF, subsequently marching from Kabul to Kandahar, in Afghanistan.

Marine Drive completes its loop on a downward gradient overlooking the Conwy Estuary and the superb backcloth of the Snowdonia National Park. Near sea level the Railway Convalescent Home occupies an impressive four-storey house styled Old Abbey, although there were never any abbots here! It had traded for many years as the Old Abbey Hotel when the Railway Convalescent Homes charity bought it for £22,500 in 1949, specifically for the use of up to 45 women. It was opened on 9 May 1950 by Lord Latham, chairman of the London Transport Executive. There was a £5,000 remodelling in 1961 and a £1.4m refurbishment and extension in 2001, to accommodate up to 52 men or women. Princess Anne, the Princess Royal, travelled to Llandudno to reopen the home on 12 October 2001, unveiling a commemorative slate plaque from Llechwedd Slate Mines, Blaenau Ffestiniog. Residents have the benefit of 15 acres of private foreshore and four acres of gardens.

Within the grounds of the convalescent home there are extensive remains of the medieval Palace of the Bishops of Bangor, built on land presented to Bishop Anian by Edward I in 1284, and sold by the church in 1891. This is what generations of residents have mistakenly called Gogarth Abbey. The surviving structure suggests the palace was built within a few years of King Edward's gift but was burnt by Owain Glyndŵr during his rebellion against the English, early in the 15th century – and never rebuilt. In the 16th century it was specifically described as a ruin. The sea has claimed much of the cliff-top site. There is a large hall, about 60 ft (18m) long and 30 ft (9m) wide, and five auxiliary rooms, with the remains of a substantial building right on the cliff edge. Items discovered on the site over the years include three silver pennies of Edward I, a limestone piscine pierced with a drain hole, and a Mediterranean style wine jar. Nothing has been done to preserve the now ivy-covered ruins, and erosion is continuous.

The Convalescent Home is possibly on the site of the Sailors' Home, Gogarth, an address inscribed on a boat-shaped tombstone at St.Tudno's church, bearing the names of Griffith Evans, died 1875, aged 75, and Thomas Evans, died 1897, aged 69.

A nearby house, called Plas Lavan, was the scene of a helicopter crash on 25 August 1968. The privately owned Brantly B2, G-ARZI, struck the cliffs and tumbled 35 feet (10.5m) down to the beach, but the pilot, Cecil Francis of Old Colwyn, and his 11-years-old son escaped with minor cuts and bruises.

The garage of St. Petrocks is all that is left of a natural chamber from which Llandudno's last cave dwellers were displaced in 1877, to make way for the new road. During the forty years they lived in the cave Miriam and Isaac Jones had reared fifteen children, including three sets of twins. Isaac, who was born at Amlwch in 1811, was seriously injured when he tried to fly by tying seagull wings to his arms and leaping into space, but Miriam nursed him back to health in the cave and the would-be Icarus lived to become an octogenarian. They refused to leave their home until the Marine Drive Company gave them a cottage, where Miriam yr Ogof (Miriam of the Cave) died in 1910, aged 91. Her many descendants are still known by what has become a family nickname, now usually anglicised and corrupted to 'Rogo.

One leaves Marine Drive to emerge at what is known as the West Shore. The old exit toll-house retains evidence of its fortification in 1940 by the local (5th Caernarvonshire) battalion of the Home Guard. Beside it there is a gate giving access to two footpaths, that on the left being an unsurfaced but well-flattened sheep walk known as the Monks' Path. It leads eventually to the summit of the Orme, its lush green colour being due to sheep droppings rather than the legendary tread of holy feet. The surfaced path on the right is known as Invalids' Walk, and leads to Haulfre Gardens although it has a zigzag spur, for the more agile, leading up to Tŷ'n-y-coed Road. A cave above the tollhouse is known as Ogof Arth, meaning Bear's Cave. The narrow entrance leads into a round chamber with a wide shelf opening out on one side. It was the home of John Stephens, a Liverpool-born farm labourer who, when interviewed by a newspaper reporter in 1862, gave his age as 31 and said he had lived there for fourteen years. Some years earlier he had been visited by Lady Mostyn who subsequently sent him an iron bed to add to his bits of furniture.

Upper Mostyn Street after the 1876 rebuilding of Tabernacl Baptist chapel. To its left is the Post Office. The present Empire Hotel is at the top of the street, while shops coming down on the right are labelled Lowe, Prichard, Hughes chemists, Burwell, and Ellerby. The 1864 Eisteddfod pavilion was built on the land in front of the chapel. One of the former Accrington Corporation trams is seen proceeding up Mostyn Street, below.

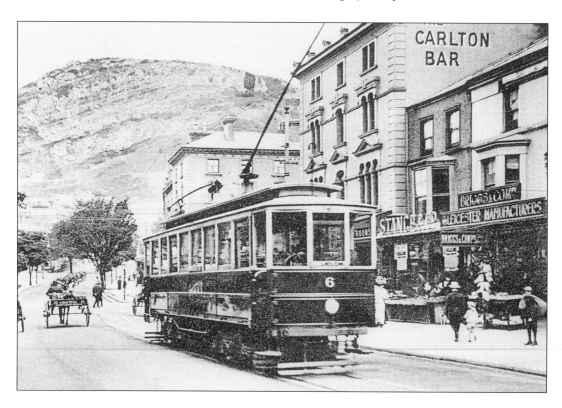

MOSTYN STREET

Mostyn Street is Llandudno's golden half-mile, once blessed with more Royal Warrants than any other shopping street outside London. As long ago as 1874 the *Liverpool Mercury* described it as being "studded on each side with many fine shops." As might be expected, the development of this thoroughfare, in a gentle arc parallel with the promenade, began in Church Walks, and that is where we shall commence our stroll in this chapter although the modern street numbering begins at the opposite end.

After but a few yards we find a by-way on the left, named Court Street, where the town's first police station was located until 1915. In their first year of office the Improvement Commissioners appointed a Dwygyfylchi man to the post of Town Constable, at a wage of 16s (80p) a week, and built a small lock-up for him in Tŷ Coch road, at a cost of £485.3s.5d. He resigned a year later and was replaced by a Ruthin man at the enhanced wage of 18s. With the creation of the Caernarvonshire Constabulary, in 1857, the Commissioners hoped to shed this burden but they were refused, as they were again in 1874 when the Chief Constable said that if Llandudno wanted a policeman, the town could afford to pay for one. By the end of the year the Chief Constable had relented and the town had its own sergeant and two constables, using an improved lock-up built in Court Street in 1867, and enlarged in 1872 to incorporate a magistrates' court. It now serves as a house – where one can still see the barred cell window.

No. 145 Mostyn Street blocks off the original road from the beach to the old village. The *Llandudno Advertiser* was printed at No.133 until the summer of 1975. It was launched on 11 April 1885 by William "Zulu" Smith, a veteran of the Zulu War of 1879, who had printed an occasional *Llandudno News Sheet* from 3 May 1882. The town's first sauna bath was opened by Urban Council chairman Algwyn Hopkins on 17 December 1968, in the basement of 127 Mostyn Street (with its entrance around the corner, in Vardre Lane). Its first users were 21-years-old dancer Halcyon Groundwater, 26-years-old teacher Gwenno Hallett, and the author – all in the interests of journalism. It enjoyed a decade or so of fashionable popularity, but became a massage parlour in the 1990s and has since closed its doors.

On the opposite side of the street we have Tabernacl Welsh Baptist chapel, founded in 1813, extended in 1836 after an appeal for funds to "Christians in rich England," and re-built in 1876 (a schoolroom being added in 1902). Its most famous minister was the Reverend Lewis Valentine, appointed in 1921 and sentenced to nine months imprisonment as one of the three Welsh nationalists who, on 8 September 1936, set fire to the contractor's stores during the building of an RAF bombing school at Penyberth, near Pwllheli (the future RAF Penrhos). He was one of the founders of the Welsh Home Rule Army (*Byddin Ymreolwyr Cymru*), which changed its name to *Plaid Genedlaethol Cymru* (Welsh Nationalist Party), under the presidency of Valentine, to provide the embryo for the present party.

Llewelyn Avenue separates the Baptist chapel from 114 Mostyn Street, built on the corner of what used to be Llysmadoc Field, where the 1864 National Eisteddfod was held in a 6,000 seat octagonal wooden pavilion. Patrons were greeted with the somewhat immodest banner: "Croesaw i Deml Athrylith – Welcome to the Temple of Genius." There was too much Welsh for the ears of Matthew Arnold, and too much English for William J. Parry, later to earn fame as militant leader of the slate quarrymen, but the mixture seemed about right for the opening president, William Bulkeley Hughes, who said: "A common idea is prevalent with regard to the keeping of these eisteddfodau. It is to the effect that it is the aim and object of those who support it so to perpetuate the Welsh language that it excludes the English. I am happy to say that that opinion is fast diminishing." History was to prove him wrong.

Masonic Hall, at No.108, is a silent memorial to the appalling poverty which used to be a winter feature at Llandudno in the days when hoteliers grew rich with the aid of cheap summer labour. It was at the rear of the Masonic Hall, in January 1895, that the town's first soup kitchen was set up, offering a bowl of soup and a lump of bread to those who could beg a penny with which to buy it. The venture was organised by a committee of women, whose minutes record gifts of coal, bones, vegetables and money. Poverty was a major problem as recently as 1934 when the Llandudno unemployed, who used to have to go to Conwy Workhouse to break their quota of stones, went on strike over having to pay 2d (a little less than a modern penny) for their mid-day meal. Masonic Street used to house the Llandudno Doll Museum opened in April 1974, with over a thousand specimens spanning four centuries and most countries of the world – and all collected by Mrs. Edith Bellamy, wife of the lifeboat coxswain.

No. 98 marks the site of a building erected in 1844 for the British & Foreign School Society. "The monitors were rude, undisciplined, and ignorant, and were neither able to teach nor to maintain discipline," said the Government inspector in 1846. The teacher was a former printer paid £47 a year (compared with £21 at the National school) but none of his pupils could read or write well. "It is difficult to conceive boys in school, and subject to a master, who are more rustic and offensive in their manners," added the inspector.

Passing the traffic roundabout, and continuing into Mostyn Street, one sees the former Café Royal and Majestic Ballroom (now a shop) on the right. This served as the recruiting depot for the 15th (1st London Welsh) Battalion of the Royal Welch Fusiliers during its raising and training in 1914.

No. 80 Mostyn Street was the first real shop of Edward Owen, butcher, of Plas Road, who established his business in 1834 in the historic boatmen's hut mentioned in Chapter 3 (More stylish than some). Sandbach's confectionery business, at 78a, was founded by two sisters in 1914. Their assistant during 1933-35 was Mary Grierson, later to become the artist at Kew Gardens where she designed two British postage stamps for a floral set issued on 24 April 1967. Farm Foods supermarket, at No.74, was built as St. George's Hall in 1864. Surprisingly perhaps, for that period, it opened with nothing less than two Mozart comic operas, *L'impresario* and *Marcellina* (both now somewhat obscure). They were performed by the Drayton Opera Company to provide the foundation for Llandudno's proud operatic tradition. St.George's Hall was modernised in 1893, and by World War One had become the Princes cinema. The D'Oyly Carte Opera appeared here in 1890, and it was within this hall that the first protest meeting against the town's leasehold system was held in 1886, at the instigation of the Reverend J. Spinther James, the well-known Baptist minister.

Dixon's shop, at 70 Mostyn Street, was opened in 1985 in what used to be a public house called The Steam Packet, and before that The Stanley. In 1965 the author was flown to France when the police reopened a three-years-old file relating to the apparent murder of one of The Stanley's barmen, Brian Painter, aged 25. He booked out of a Kenilworth hotel on 23 October 1962, and a few minutes later £400 was found to be missing from the safe, as was a car from the car park, which was later found abandoned at Dover. French police have a huge network of informers, and on 25 October Painter's description was accurately noted at the Luxy Cabaret Club, in Paris, together with his generosity to a prostitute named Giselle, who helped him spend on a lavish scale. He left the club, and a Triumph TR2 car that had been parked in the nearby Rue Reaumur vanished. Twelve hours and a hundred miles (161km) later police logged the TR2 outside a café on the outskirts of Troyes, but did not know it was stolen. At midnight, that same day, more informers saw him leave a nightclub at Troyes. On the afternoon of the 27th Painter and a pretty girl were seen to leave a café in a TR2. One-and-half hours later the Mayor of Bouy-Luxembourg was in one of his fields when he saw a TR2 negotiating a muddy lane into a spinney. He also saw a Citroen parked in the spinney. Next day a game hunter found Painter's body lying behind the stolen TR2. The ignition key was missing. Three years later the French police made some arrests but the investigation never came to anything.

On the opposite side of this section of the street No.111 was the Dunphy family's high-class grocery store from 1857 until January 1972. Irish-born Mrs. Dunphy founded the business in 1850 by baking muffins at 20 Back Mostyn Street, an address that has now become 14 Somerset Street. Their next bakehouse and warehouse was in Market Street where the first-floor was held up by unmistakable ships' masts and spars, including a main jib boom complete with its "cheeks" for pivoting on a mast. They had been collected off the beach in the days when wrecks were plentiful, and pressed into service as builders' timber. Some of these readily identifiable ship's timbers were reused when the bakehouse was demolished to be replaced in 1981 by the present Cottage Loaf Inn.

It was to Dunphy's shop that Llandudno's first coloured immigrant came as a storeman at the turn of the century. He was Joe Taylor who married and settled down after arriving in the area with a travelling fair. A gap in the roof of W. H. Smith's shop, at No. 101 (best seen from the rear) is the last vestige of an old footpath to the sea.

As the headquarters of Wartski, the Royal jewellers, from 1928 until February 1972, No. 93 Mostyn Street (now Goldsmiths) was a truly remarkable shop – and there is still a sign in London's Grafton Street (off Bond Street) stating: "Wartski of Llandudno." Morris Wartski arrived at 21 High Street, Bangor in 1882 as a 27-years-old refugee from Poland. Two of his sons, Charles and Harry, who were born at Bangor, moved to Llandudno in 1909 to open a shop at 33 Mostyn Street, followed, two years later, by a branch in London's Bond Street. In 1928 the Llandudno shop moved to 93 Mostyn Street, and a year later the Bond Street shop moved to 138 Regent Street. In 1970 Kenneth Snowman, a grandson of Morris Wartski, decided Regent Street had become "a bit rough" and moved to 14 Grafton Street. After the Bolshevik Revolution members of the Wartski family toured Europe, looking up exiled Russian aristocrats from whom they bought the fabulous *objets d'art* made by Carl Fabergé, jeweller to the Tsars. In 1925 they scooped the world and bought the bulk of the Tsar's personal jewellery from the Soviet government. This was the basis of their numerous Royal Warrants and the Coats of Arms that used to be displayed over the Llandudno shop, to denote that their customers included Queen Alexandra, King George V, Queen Mary, Queen Elizabeth (consort of King George VI), and Queen Elizabeth II, as well as members of the Danish and Greek royal families. As Jews one of their most spectacular ventures was when they went to revolutionary Egypt in 1954 to buy up the Fabergé collection of King Farouk, who had been deposed by his army in 1952.

Arnold's Store once occupied 83/85 Mostyn Street. It was founded in 1882 by William Arnold, a Norfolk grocer who arrived to manage a small drapery shop adjacent to what became the family business. He was eventually joined by his son Clement Arnold who, after winning the DSO in World War One, joined the local unit of the Territorial Army to become commanding officer of the 69th Medium Regiment, Royal Artillery, by the time they were

Still readily recognisable at the corner of Mostyn Street and Tudno Street, the grocery shop of Tenby & Son was also the London & North Western Railway parcels office. St.George's Hall, in Mostyn Street, was the first North Wales opera house. Below are politician John Bright and actors Sir Alec Guinness and Glynis Johns on Llandudno promenade for the filming of The Card in 1951.

mobilised for World War Two. After he returned from the war he gave the store a new frontage, to make it one of the most famous stores in North Wales. It was again upgraded in 1972, but Lieut-Colonel Arnold died in December 1978, and Arnold's store closed at the end of 1989.

Crossing the intersection with Lloyd Street we arrive at the Milk Bar at 69 Mostyn Street, where the town's first telephone exchange was opened in an attic in 1892, at the request of a Dr. Freer who asked the National Telephone Company to provide a service between his home and his promenade surgery. The exchange closed in 1927 when Llandudno became one of the first towns to have an automatic system, wired to new equipment at Colwyn Bay. Marks & Spencer opened at 61 Mostyn Street in 1936, when no item cost more than 5s (25p), e.g. a smart woman's raincoat was one penny less than 5s. The shop was extended in 1972, when the first North Wales escalators came into use. There were further extensions in 2000. Their shop includes the site of the Manse that belonged to St. John's English Wesleyan church opened in 1866 – after moving from their first church erected in 1861 in Lloyd Street. In 1989 St. John's schoolroom was demolished to make way for a second Marks & Spencer store, developed on the site of the once famous Bunney's Corner store, demolished in November and December 1987. The church remains in use between the two shops.

The Savoy cinema stood at No.35 until its demolition in 1987. It was designed by Arthur Hewitt and opened in August 1914, on the site of the former Royal Oak Hotel. It was re-built, without its balcony, in 1956 after a serious fire. One of the new owners was Eric Johnson (son-in-law of local architect Arthur Hewitt), a very tall local accountant, whose daughter Dorothy once told the author how he declared this would be one cinema where he could always sit in comfort – resulting in wide spacing between the rows of seats.

Retracing our steps, to take a look at the opposite side of the street, the HSBC Bank (formerly the Midland Bank) at No.68 occupies a corner where R. Roberts & Son, The Royal Fish Stores, once had a shop, before moving along into Lloyd Street, They were founded in 1854 and used to proclaim across the front of their Lloyd Street premises: "Purveyors of fish to the Royal Court of Roumania" well into the 1960s, a relic of the Queen of Romania's holiday at Llandudno in 1890.

This fishy claim to fame was in answer to the cast-iron boast across the front of No. 56: "Sole makers of the Royal Sandringham Sausage. John Jones, Royal Butcher." During Queen Victoria's visit to Pale, near Bala, in 1889, he announced he had received a special order to supply her with Welsh mutton and his patent Royal Sandringham Sausages. However his Royal Warrant was considerably older for he was advertising himself as the Queen's Butcher in the first *Llandudno News Sheet* of 1882. His ornate sign survived, in excellent condition, until 1960.

Until 1994 part of No.56 housed the El Alamein Club, named by the Llandudno branch of the Royal Artillery Association in 1971, to commemorate the turning point in the history of the local regiment in World War Two (see chapter 13, Wormhout Way).

The present Public Library was opened in 1910, on the site of an earlier single-storey Newsroom and Library founded in 1873 on the initiative of Lady Augusta Mostyn. The foundation stone was laid on 14 October 1873 by William Bulkeley Hughes, MP. One of its regular users and subscribers was politician John Bright who, when staying in the town, would call every day to read *The Times*. It was a privately funded operation, relying on subscriptions, and when it became obvious that Llandudno needed something better Mostyn Estates agent George Alfred Humphreys arranged for library philanthropist Andrew Carnegie and John Walker, of Osborne House, on Llandudno's North Parade to fund the present building, to be run by Llandudno Urban District Council. It opened in 1910, and there were extensive additions during 1938-39. The pillared façade and much of the original interior has been preserved in the present 1992 extension.

Next to the Library stands the new Victoria Shopping Centre, opened in 1992 to replace a particularly ugly block of shops built a quarter of a century earlier on the site of Zion English Baptist chapel. The chapel was erected in 1862 and demolished in 1967 when Mostyn Estates refused to renew the lease, stating the high street was no place for chapels. A tree planted in the grounds in 1877 to commemorate the chapel's first wedding survived on the post-1967 pavement until 1997, when it fell victim to Dutch Elm Disease. The rubble from the demolished Zion chapel was used to make road foundations for a new Council housing estate beside Conwy Road.

In 1996 Cinema 100, an organisation set up to celebrate the centenary of cinematography in Britain, affixed a plaque to the outside Library wall to commemorate John Codman, a son of Punch & Judy pioneer Richard Codman. It was unveiled by John Codman's great niece Jacqueline Millband. He went into the new film industry at the very outset and by August 1896 was presenting his own programme of animated pictures in the music halls, later moving on to touring Wales and Lancashire with his mobile cinema, hauled by a steam traction engine. His films, such as *Launching of HM Battleship King Edward VII* and *Scenes from the Passion Play at Oberammergau* (filmed by himself) were interspersed with songs by his sisters Naomi and Florence. He also established some fixed early cinemas, although Llandudno's first cinematograph show was provided by the Pier Company, in July 1900, at their Bijou Theatre, next door to the Pavilion, using "the American biograph machine."

Holy Trinity church, which will become the parish church in 2002, stands in its own lawn lower down Mostyn Street. The foundation stone, laid in 1865, bears an inscription stating that the ceremony was performed by Lady Augusta Mostyn. In fact Lady Augusta was ill and the stone was laid by Mrs. Katherine Anwyl Morgan, wife of the Rector. Beneath the stone there is a large bottle containing a newspaper, a local guidebook and coins of the period. Holy Trinity, which has 1,200 seats, was consecrated and first used for worship in July 1874, and a new chancel was added in 1932. The tower contains a peel of eight bells given by Herbert Keeling and his wife Caroline, of Tudno Villa (now St.Tudno Hotel), who died in 1893 and 1892 respectively.

The Colours of the 13th and 17th Battalions, Royal Welch Fusiliers, were laid up at Holy Trinity in 1919 – when a German machine-gun was presented to the public library for permanent public display. The War Memorial chapel was created in 1924, with three marble wall plaques listing the 219 local men killed in World War One. The stained glass window in the chapel is inscribed: "To the memory of the Officers, Non-Commissioned Officers and Men of the 17th Bn. RWF (raised at Llandudno) who fell in the War 1914-18. The gift of their Commanding Officer, Colonel the Hon. H.T Lloyd Mostyn, 1934." It incorporates the figure of St.Cadwaladr and the regimental badge.

Behind the east end of Holy Trinity, in Trinity Square, one can explore the Alice in Wonderland Centre, opened in May 1987 by Muriel and Murray Ratcliffe. A walk through the centre takes the visitor on an exceptionally well laid out underground tour of animated Wonderland, in virtually any language, to re-emerge in an informative exhibition of Alice artefacts. These include 46 figures based on the original *Alice in Wonderland* drawings of John Tenniel, carved over a period of two years by Japanese audio animatronics engineer Takashi Ohe. They were carved as part of his art degree course at Tokyo University, after which he decided Llandudno's Alice in Wonderland centre was the most appropriate place to house them.

In 1860 John Hughes established a well-known fish and poultry business at 12 Mostyn

Street. It passed through three generations, the last being Enoch Hughes who created a novel export business for French gourmets. In 1953 he began experimenting in storing live lobsters in big tanks in the basement, for use as an unusual Christmas delicacy at local hotels. He expanded into supplying the best hotels in Paris. Upon receipt of a telephone order he would pack the lobsters in wet sawdust for delivery, still alive, by road and air via Manchester. By 1967 he could handle several hundred lobsters a day in the catching season, most of them coming from Cardigan Bay. His daughter is Mrs. Elizabeth Maddocks, of the Empire Hotel.

Officially known as North Western Gardens, the small park at the intersection of Mostyn Street with Vaughan Street has been described for decades as Lavatory Island, a reminder of its underground conveniences. This facility was retained when the garden received a £400,000 Heritage Lottery fund upgrade in 1999. In order to provide access for the disabled a lift was installed with what looks suspiciously like a *Dr. Who* space vehicle on the surface. The slender column, resembling a cross between an industrial stovepipe and a Red Indian totem pole, is a £20,000 sculpture by Craig and Mary Matthews, intended to encapsulate the history of the town. The name North Western Gardens is a reminder that the Tudno Castle Hotel opposite was known for many years as the North Western Hotel – a name derived from the London & North Western Railway (LNWR), who operated the nearby station until the company lost its identity in the January 1923 grouping that gave us the London, Midland & Scottish Railway (LMS).

After the intersection with Vaughan Street the town's main artery changes its name to Mostyn Broadway, a road slowly opened up during 1905-07. The large furniture store in what had served until 1980 as an Electricity Board showroom was built after World War One as a ballroom. Later it became a roller-skating rink and then a garage.

Llandudno's 33-metre swimming pool was opened in August 1973, after 61 years of debate by the Urban Council as to how much it was to cost and where it should go. It was in 1912 that the Council began discussing a replacement for the former pool beneath the Pier Pavilion. Twenty years later they offered three prizes, each of 50 guineas, for the best pool plan, but dropped the idea in 1934, when the private enterprise West Shore Lido was opened, with an open air pool 225 ft (69m) long and 120 ft (36m) wide. After a decade of national fame for its bathing beauty contests, run by town Publicity Association secretary Ted Williams during summer weekends, the Lido closed in 1959 and was demolished in 1963 to make way for flats. That prompted the Council to return to the idea and plans were prepared for what would have been one of the finest pools in Britain, with lockers for 640 bathers, a public gallery, sun lounge, indoor water garden, restaurants and a bar. Because of the uncertainties surrounding the impending 1974 reorganisation of local government, after which Llandudno would no longer control its own destiny but would have a minority of only 15 councillors among the 41 on the new Aberconwy Council, a cheaper and quicker scheme was sought. The result is today's rather small pool, partially funded with £50,000 raised in a town lottery promoted by Councillor Jim Williams, of the Richmond Hotel (now the Ambassador).

The 1,100-seat three-tier Grand Theatre opened on 5 August 1901, six long years before the road linking it to either Llandudno or Craig-y-don, beside a muddy track known only as "Mostyn Street extension." Understandably, it had a poor start in life. Its first manager was none less than Milton Bode, who took it on a short lease, and left after two years to run the Theatre Royal, Northampton, with the formidable Edward Compton. Matching Llandudno's well-established musical tradition, the Grand recruited a good full-time orchestra. It remained open winter and summer, with a mixture of repertory and light variety. One of the musicians who joined the orchestra in 1920 was black clarinetist Edmund Jenkins. His father, a Baptist minister, ran an orphanage in Charleston, South Carolina, famous for its Jenkins' Orphanage Band. Edmund Jenkins won numerous awards at the Royal Academy of Music before turning up at Llandudno, and he is still remembered in America as a composer, although his life was cut short by an early death in 1926.

A season of grand opera was staged at the Grand in 1926, by the O'Mara Company. It played to near full houses for a repertory of *Il Trovatore, Carmen, Maritana, Daughter of the Regiment, Tannhäuser* and *Bohemian Girl.* The company returned the following year with *Carmen, Tales of Hoffman, Rigoletto* and *Il Trovatore.*

Renamed the Broadway nightclub in July 1987, the old Grand Theatre is a memorial to the commercial miscalculation of a local company floated in 1899, in every anticipation of an early merging of Llandudno and Craig-y-don. The two Victorian conurbations were separated by green fields and an ancient artificial and invisible parish and Episcopal boundary – one in the diocese of Bangor and the other in the diocese of St.Asaph. They built their West End theatre in miniature in a field behind Rivière's Concert Hall, which was to have been the focal point for a new pier. This was planned to be a new 20th century entertainment complex, to outshine anything else in the Queen of the Welsh Resorts. Like the rest of the building, the cleverly engineered stage with adjustable rake, had been designed by Edwin O. Sachs, restorer of Covent Garden and world famous for his stages – but G.A. Humphreys, architect and agent to Mostyn Estates, claimed much of the credit for the architecture. It was linked directly to the promenade by Irving Road until 1980, when the local authority blocked it off to provide parking space for the Sailing Club.

The Grand's greatest days were during World War Two, when it was taken over by the evacuated BBC Variety Department for a series of regular shows, including *Happidrome,* announced as "Coming to you from somewhere in Britain." Run by Ernest Longstaff, its chief comic was Harry Korris, the "Mr.Lovejoy" of the show, who would lead the singing of the opening and closing song: "Just a set of twerps like we, Ramsbottom, and Enoch and me." He was familiar with Llandudno, having performed at the Happy Valley in 1923 and 1924, and also at the Palladium. Tommy Handley's famous *ITMA* radio show moved from Bangor to Llandudno in 1943, and the Grand was the venue for its 100th performance. This was also the first evacuated home of the BBC theatre organ, which played for hour after hour during the early years of the war, to fill up radio time during a period of depleted resources. The organ was later moved to the County Theatre, Bangor, and after the war was sold to the Pasadena Civic Auditorium, California, where it is still in use.

The Welsh National Opera gave their first North Wales season at the Grand in September 1951 – after they had cleared out the manure, straw and smell of their predecessors, the Circus Rosaire. The infant company had been given special funding to travel out of Cardiff as part of the Festival of Britain celebrations. Their unadvertised season of *Il Trovatore, Cavalleria Rusticana & Pagliacci,* and *Madam Butterfly* was already half-way through before the *Llandudno Advertiser* caught up, describing them as a company of miners, factory workers, professional and businessman – a reminder of the amateur chorus which served the WNO with enthusiasm and distinction until as recently as 1973. The 1951 *ad hoc* orchestra of 27 was made up largely of BBC musicians from Cardiff. By the time the WNO returned to Llandudno six years later the company had grown too big for this intimate stage (see Chapter 14, Gloddaeth Street). An arsonist seriously damaged the superbly engineered stage of the then derelict Grand Theatre on 26 December 1985.

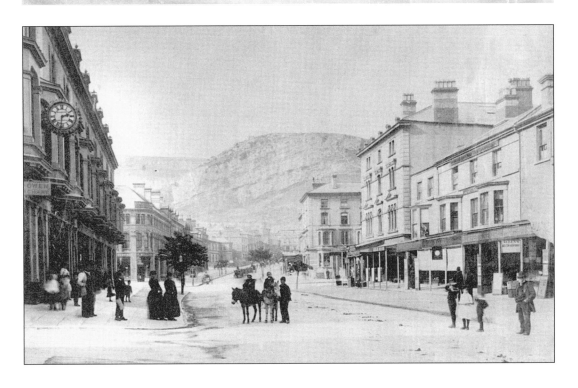

Mostyn Street before the advent of the motorcar. Like the Pied Piper of Hamelin, the town band is seen parading down the street in 1914, recruiting volunteers for Lloyd George's Welsh Army.

Mostyn Arms stood beside Llanrhos church until 1897.

Llandudno's first Welsh language primary school was founded in 1949 in wartime Army Nissen huts beside Conwy Road.

CONWY ROAD & LLANRHOS

12

Conwy Road, forming a junction with the eastern end of Mostyn Street, was opened in 1844 as an alternative to the only other route from Llanrhos, which was via Fferm Bach Road and Nant-y-gamar Road down to the beach. It was laid by public subscription of labour, materials and money on a strip of marshland given by the then owner of Gloddaeth, Lady Champneys (née Charlotte Mostyn, b.1768) – the widow of a spendthrift Somerset baronet, Sir Thomas Swymmer Champneys, 1769-1839.

By 1891 the popularity of Llandudno was such that the land at the rear of the Tudno Castle Hotel was surveyed as the terminal site for a new line the Midland Railway Company proposed to tunnel through the Little Orme, in opposition to the marginally longer route of the London & North Western Railway Company. A 50,000 square feet (4645sqm) Asda superstore, with parking space for 643 cars, was opened on this site in April 1975, swallowing up the football field and stand, a coach park, a showground, allotments and some wasteland. Asda came to Llandudno by invitation. The company, which then had a Caernarfon-born chief executive, had intended building the first North Wales supermarket in Rhyl, where the chamber of trade persuaded the local council that such a venture should be sited as far as possible from the town centre, so as to reduce the competition. Llandudno chamber of trade was somewhat wiser, and in conjunction with Llandudno Urban Council invited Asda to the town on condition that it came as close as possible to the town centre, with a general-purpose car park not restricted to Asda customers, so as to supplement Llandudno's famous shopping tradition. Neighbouring Colwyn Bay Borough Council opposed the plan, but that was interpreted as sour grapes. The first Asda store was destroyed by fire on 27 August 1976, but was rebuilt to reopen a year later. The retail site was expanded eastwards during 1988-89 to accommodate numerous supermarkets which, with the traditional town centre shopping streets, make Llandudno the envy of North Wales.

Argyll Road, running off Conwy Road, parallel to Vaughan Street, contains the old Drill Hall of the Territorial Army, where 242 Battery of the 61st (Caernarvon & Denbigh Yeomanry) Medium Regiment, Royal Garrison Artillery was formed in 1921, when the Denbighshire Hussars were amalgamated with 1/1 Welsh (Caernarvonshire) Royal Garrison Artillery. The 69th (Caernarvon & Denbigh Yeomanry) Medium Regiment was raised at Llandudno Drill Hall, out of 242 Battery, and as a separate volunteer force in July 1939. In 1947 the 61st and 69th Regiments were merged to form 361st Medium Regiment, RA (Caernarvon & Denbigh Yeomanry), Territorial Army. This regiment was, in turn, merged in 1956 with 384 Light Regiment, RA (RWF) TA, to form 372 (Flintshire & Denbighshire Yeomanry) Regiment, RA, TA. Llandudno's last gun, a 25-pounder, left the Drill Hall in September 1966, and 372 Regiment was disbanded in April 1967.

Llandudno's Volunteer tradition dated from the American-led French invasion of Fishguard, in Cardigan Bay, on 22 February 1797. The French plan was to recruit a Foreign Legion of disaffected Welshmen to join them in a march on Chester and Liverpool, but the over-optimistic invaders surrendered two days later. Learning of the scheme, the Reverend Edward Edwards, Rector of Llanrwst, wrote to the Home Secretary (the Duke of Portland) on 27 February, stating: "The fear of pillage and plunder of a rich and happy spot of the Principality of North Wales forces me to address your Grace. There are strong suspicions of an intention in the enemy of attempting a descent in Llandudno or Llandrillo Bay, or both, the first lying between the Great and Little Orme's head and the other immediately east of them. I have explained the motive of my fear to Thomas Williams, Esquire, Member for Great Marlow [i.e. Thomas Williams, MP, of Llanidan and Marl, owner of Conwy ferry] than whom I know no person more adequate to specify to your Grace the true state of that part of Wales. Sir Thomas Mostyn and Mr. Williams, in case of a landing effected, will inevitably be the first and principal sufferers. The coast is extremely defenceless: no military nearer than Denbigh (20 miles), and those ye Roxborough Fencibles. Llandudno Bay is a fine bay full in the face of the North wind, little or no sand at low water and a very bold shore. It is presumed that a frigate of force stationed between Linsy Point [i.e. Point Lynas] in Anglesey and the Isle of Man would more effectively protect the coast than a great land force. A cutter was heretofore always upon this station.

"In the meantime I have suggested to a magistrate near Denbigh that a party of the Fencibles traversing along the coast from St. Asaph to Conwy would be of service, eventually, if it was consistent with their duty to be absent from Denbigh."

Promptly replying, on 1 March, the Home Secretary said the matter was being referred to the Duke of York, Commander in Chief, adding: "Your anxiety for the safety of your country cannot but be highly praiseworthy and you may depend upon His Majesty's Ministers paying every possible attention to the security of the county in which you reside."

The military situation in North Wales was even worse than the Rector thought, for the Roxburgh and Selkirk Cavalry (Fencibles) had left Denbigh by June 1796. Agitation caused by the Fishguard invasion prompted the raising of a regiment of Llandudno Volunteers, one of whose efficiency medals, oval and made of solid gold, turned up in a London antique shop in 1959. The obverse is inscribed "Llandudno Volunteers 1801," surrounding an engraving of a rifleman whose cap is adorned with a fusilier's hackle. The reverse is inscribed: "Award of merit to Henry Lewis, Esq., as a token of his efficiency in the cause of the Llandudno Volunteers, 12th July 1801." The 1801 census tells us Llandudno then had a population of only 318. There is a tombstone in Llanrhos churchyard for Robert Jones, aged 52, buried in August 1805 and described as "lieutenant of the Isdulas Volunteers and former paymaster and sergeant-major of the Caernarvonshire Militia." At some stage Llandudno raised men for the Carnarvonshire Yeomanry Cavalry, a regiment absorbed in 1885 by the Denbighshire Hussars Yeomanry. Called up at very short notice in January 1900, the Llandudno Troop served with the 29th (Denbighshire) Company of the Imperial Yeomanry, raised to fight in the Boer War, losing one man killed in action and another due to an unspecified African disease. Two more men from Llandudno succumbed to disease while serving with the 3rd Volunteer Battalion of the Royal Welch Fusiliers. After the war the Caernarvonshire elements of the cavalry were grouped to form C Squadron of the Denbighshire Hussars, which was absorbed into the new Territorial Army in 1908. Posted to Egypt in World War One, the Hussars were dismounted to form the 24th (Denbigh Yeomanry) Battalion of the Royal Welch Fusiliers, after

Llanrhos church, showing the private gateway on the right for the Mostyn family at Gloddaeth and Bodysgallen.

which they fought their way into Palestine with the 74th (Yeomanry) Division – whose divisional sign was a broken spur. The 74th Division later served in France.

At opposite ends of Argyll Road stand the Llandudno Health Centre, opened in January 1965, and the building it replaced, the former War Memorial Child Welfare Centre (and upstairs maternity home), opened on 26 November 1926 by future Prime Minister Neville Chamberlain, the then Minister of Health. The modern Health Centre was built on land that had been occupied since 1940 by corrugated iron Nissen huts, erected for the Army. It was in these huts that the town's first Welsh-language primary school was opened in 1949, remaining there until it moved in 1963 into a new building beside the River Creuddyn (culverted in 1973), in Cwm Road. Another of the huts was taken over in 1952 for the foundation of the Llandudno Hotel & Catering School, which opened with eight students, to be absorbed in 1964 in the new Llandrillo Technical College. The 1926 maternity home is now Oxford House Clinic, opened in 2000 for physiotherapy and alternative medicine.

Llandudno's Fire Station, on the left of Conwy Road, was opened in March 1970 to replace the original 1877 station. Among the relics preserved inside is a heavy brass bell inscribed "Llandudno Fire Bell 1861," which spent most of its life at the end of the Pier, until removed during the construction of the present landing stage in 1969. It originally hung from a frame beside the pony-stand outside the Market Hall, where a notice said it was to be rung by anyone discovering a fire. How it got to the Pier is a mystery. A five-man volunteer fire brigade was formed at Llandudno as long ago as 1854, equipped with ladders and hose which were later stored in a vault beneath the market. Agitation for something better began in 1874 and three years later a horse-drawn Merryweather hand pump was installed in a new building in Market Street. This was replaced by a steam pump, formally christened the *St. Tudno*, in 1882, and which served until the arrival of a petrol driven fire engine in 1925.

The Links Hotel has an interesting origin. It was opened in 1898 by Sam Hughes, secretary of the Llandudno Pier Company, on a freehold plot given to him by Lady Augusta Mostyn in exchange for his family home, the Mostyn Arms – an inn which stood opposite the 1820 lych-gate of Llanrhos church. The presence of the Mostyn Arms on one side of the church, and the Queen's Head on the other, offended Lady Augusta's ideals and she arranged for the closure of both, leaving only the Cocoa House (later the sub-post office) across the road. The Links was built beside an ancient footpath, traces of which can still be identified, running from Nant-y-gamar to West Shore.

The section west of the hotel has now become Maesdu Road where the town's first gasometer was installed in 1857, beside the gas works bought by the Improvement Commissioners in 1876, and extended two years later, with two chimneys 42 ft (12.8m) high. A second gasometer was built in 1899, and with a capacity of 500,000 cubic feet (14150cum) was the largest in North Wales. It remained in use until 1948 and was demolished ten years later. Another gasometer, again the biggest in North Wales, was built on the opposite side of Maesdu road in 1932 with a capacity of a million cubic feet (28300cum). The gas industry was nationalised in 1949, at which time there were 33 separate producers in North Wales. In 1956 the Gas Board introduced the North Wales gas grid, drawing methane from Point of Ayr colliery and coke-oven gas from Shotton steelworks, coupled with a new coal gas works at Maelor, Wrexham. All other gas works in the region were then closed and dismantled. North Sea gas was introduced into the system in 1969 and the total conversion was completed in 1971.

In 1898 the Urban Council built a combined refuse incinerator and steam turbine for electricity generation, beside the gas works. Refuse was burnt to raise steam for three dynamos. The electrical engineer for the scheme was Arthur Henry Preece (later knighted), 31-years-old son of Caernarfon wireless pioneer Sir William Preece. The project was designed to light 50 street lamps, but was to be developed in stages over a period of a year (starting in July 1898) for a maximum output to supply 10,000 eight-candlepower lamps. The 150 ft (46m) high power-station chimney, ornately fashioned out of red Ruabon bricks, was demolished in October 1971. Another tall chimney in this area belonged to the former Llandudno Brick, Lime & Stone Company.

No. 6 Cwm Place, off Maesdu Road, was the last home of Llandudno's oldest citizen, Rose Stallard, who died on 4 April 1972, three months short of her 103rd birthday. Herself the mother of eleven children, she left 158 direct descendants. On her 100th birthday she told the author how, as a child, she earned her keep by carrying buckets of water from the sea to various hotels, for visitors to bathe their feet. She was paid a flat rate of 2d (less than 1p) a bucketful, no matter what the state of the tide, i.e. the distance she had to carry the water. One of her earliest recollections was of having the exiled Emperor Napoleon III pointed out to her when she was a very young child. He died soon afterwards but was talked about for years, she said.

The Gwydyr Road area, bounded by Conwy Road and Maesdu Road, was used as an aerodrome from 1925, when a salesman for an oil company used to land here. Travelling flying circuses used it in the 1930s and it was also the base of Llandudno Flying Club whose hangar now serves as a garage in Cwm Road. In 1934 this land was the venue for the only visit to Llandudno of the Royal Welsh Agricultural Show, which attracted an attendance of 37,323. The prizewinners included King George V, with a bull and a heifer from his Windsor herd of Shorthorns. Proceeding along Conwy Road we arrive at the original route into town at what is now the top of Queen's Road. On the opposite side we have Vicarage Road – taking its name not from the present Llanrhos Vicarage, on the corner, but the much larger 1903 building at the top left which, in November 1973, was opened as a Franciscan friary, within the Anglican Communion. It was dedicated by the Archbishop of Wales, and the congregation included four bishops. The chapel contained a carved wooden statue of St. Francis, originally housed in the first Welsh Franciscan hostel that was opened at Ffestiniog in 1931, for the care of tramps during an era of economic depression and unemployment. When the Ffestiniog lease expired the Franciscans moved into Cors-y-gedol, near Barmouth, closing in 1939 when World War Two absorbed all the unemployed. The statue was then placed for safe custody in the Church Hostel, Bangor, from where it was moved to Llandudno in 1973. The European Chapter of the Order of St. Francis closed the friary in 1983, when the statue was given a permanent home in a new Franciscan chapel within St.Paul's Church, Craig-y-don.

At its eastern end Conwy Road now forks left to Wormhout Way, a link road opened in 1985 as part of the A470 Llandudno Promenade to Cardiff Docks, North to South Wales trunk road, and to the A55 expressway. The original road forks right into Llanrhos.

The historic mansion of Gloddaeth originally stood hidden at the end of a long drive, behind Llanrhos church, but today's access is from Wormhout Way. The estate came into the possession of the Mostyn family through the marriage, in 1460, of Howel ab Ieuan Fychan to Margaret, daughter of Gruffydd ap Rhys ap Gruffydd ap Madoc Gloddaeth ap Madoc ab Iorwerth Goch of Creuddyn – the latter name containing a pedigree of six generations, and probably spanning the period to just before the English conquest of 1284. Of the present house, occupied since 1965 by the boys of St. David's College, the oldest part is the Great Hall, a handsome structure of the mid-16th century with the addition of a 17th century gallery. The remainder was built at the end of the 17th century and there are also some modern buildings at the rear. A building to the east of the house is inscribed "RM 1770" but was renovated in 1897 and converted in 1935 into a school assembly room. It was seriously damaged by fire on 27 October 1975.

Llandudno's dominant Mostyn family mansions, Gloddaeth (above),
now a school, and Bodysgallen, now a hotel.

In 1970 St. David's temporarily became the fictional Chantrey School for the film *Unman, Wittering and Zigo,* starring David Hemmings and his wife Gayle Hunnicutt. The plot involved the mysterious cliff-top murder of a teacher, and some scenes were filmed on both the Great Orme and Little Orme.

St. David's College is not the first school to occupy the house. From 1935 until the end of 1964 it was the home of Gloddaeth Hall School for Girls, which was founded in 1892 at Arnhall, St. Annes, by Miss Agnes Hall and Miss Emma Gibb. In 1913 the founders moved to a big building in Bryn-y-Bia Road, Llandudno, which they called Arnhall. When the founders retired in 1923 the school was bought by two of the teachers, Miss Agnes Moffat and Miss Emma Hill, who changed the name when they moved into Gloddaeth Hall in 1935, producing a new prospectus stating: "If their parents so desire, the girls may hunt with the Flint & Denbigh hounds." It was at Gloddaeth Hall that the school reached its peak of 130 boarders and 68 day girls, but in the Spring of 1964 the headmistress told the author: "It is the unanimous view of the governors that the falling number of pupils and lack of intake of new girls makes it quite impossible to carry on."

St. David's College took over the house a year later. It was founded as a boys' school by Ormskirk-born John Mayor, aged 37, who was not himself the product of a public school or a university graduate, and Liverpool businessman Lewis Edwards, a descendant of the famous Reverend Thomas Charles, and great nephew of the first Principal of the University College of Wales, Aberystwyth (Thomas Charles Edwards). Mr. Edwards had stood as Labour candidate for Ormskirk at the 1950 general election, and for West Derby division of Liverpool in 1951. The two men went in search of a building in North Wales and chanced upon Gloddaeth Hall just as the girls were about to depart.

"Lord Mostyn was not very happy with the idea of letting lots of boys loose in place of genteel young ladies, but he was persuaded to agree to the transfer of the lease," Mr. Mayor told the author.

"We signed all the necessary documents in March 1965, at which time our only money was an overdraft guaranteed by the bank. I worked at Kingsmead Preparatory School, Hoylake, until July and issued a prospectus announcing the opening of St. David's in September. I was married and we had five children. I was leaving a comfortable safe job for this new venture in what was really a foreign land, for Wales was largely unknown to me," said Mr. Mayor, adding that he had faith in Divine guidance. To his relief the school opened with 38 boys and four teachers – the first to enrol being Jonathan Jeffrey, of Llandudno – and soon became a great success.

The other great Mostyn house now accessed from the link road is Bodysgallen. After the death in 1966 of its bachelor owner, Ievan Lloyd Mostyn, Bodysgallen was sold a year later, with a fabulous three-day auction of the contents that had accumulated over several centuries. They included a four-poster bed used by Queen Elisabeth of Romania (Carmen Sylva) after a dinner party in 1890. The other guests for that dinner were the Duke and Duchess of Teck (parents of the future Queen Mary), Lord & Lady Mostyn, Lady Augusta Mostyn, Colonel Henry Mostyn and his wife Georgina, Miss Hélène Vacaresco (the Queen's travelling companion), and G.A. Humphreys, agent to the Mostyn Estate, with Mrs. Humphreys. The Royal harpist John Thomas (Pencerdd Gwalia) was present to entertain the guests. Thereafter reserved for a possible return visit by the Balkan queen, the bed was never used again and the room in which she had slept was kept locked – used only to store a mound of wedding presents, still in their original wrapping, given for the marriage in 1883 of Henry Mostyn (brother of the 3rd Baron Mostyn) to the Hon. Pamela Georgina Douglas Pennant, 20-years-old daughter of Lord Penrhyn. On a hook, in the 17th century main hall, hung an officer's satchel of the

Caernarvonshire Militia, tossed there when one of the family returned from the regiment's final parade in 1908, after the colours were laid up in Christ Church, Caernarfon (now a children's play centre). Incredible though it may seem today, Bodysgallen was sold for £15,000 in 1967, and has since been developed into one of Britain's best hotels. Its contents were auctioned for a total of £35,000. In the garden there is a pet's grave bearing the inscription: "Miss Frances Mostyn's faithful Funny died April 17th, 1820, aged about ten years."

Eglwys Rhos, or Llanrhos church, was rebuilt in 1865 but incorporates much of the original medieval structure, including the main roof beams. Maelgwn Gwynedd is credited with having established the church in about 550 AD, at the same time as he created the Bishopric of Bangor. In 546 AD the Welsh tribal chieftains elected him King of all the Britons and he reigned from the fortified twin peaks of nearby Deganwy. During the "yellow pestilence," said to have been caused by a multitude of unburied bodies lying around, he sought refuge in the church but one day peeped through the keyhole and caught the fatal disease. He may have been buried in his church.

The church houses a heavy tombstone providing evidence of a well-established Christian presence in Llandudno round about AD 600, coinciding with the date ascribed to St. Tudno's arrival on the Great Orme. It is an inscribed boulder, first mentioned (by Lewis Morris) in 1731, and rediscovered a century later forming part of a pigsty wall at Tyddyn Holland, a farm beside Bodafon Lane. It was then removed to the roadside, from where it was taken to the church in 1908 (although the site was actually in the parish of Llandudno until 1933). The stone is 37$\frac{1}{2}$ inches (95cm) high and its abbreviated Latin inscription is of a style used around AD 600. There have been several conflicting interpretations of the inscription, the current favourite being SANCTANUS SACERDOS IN PACE, meaning "Sanctinus the Bishop in peace." It has been suggested that Sanctanus might be Santagnus, which would convert into Welsh as Sannan. The church contains separate vaults for some of the early graves of the Gloddaeth, Bodysgallen, Penrhyn and Marl families. The walls are adorned with several memorials to members of the Mostyn family, including one that tells us Colonel Hugh Wynne, of Bodysgallen, raised, at his own expense, a regiment of foot soldiers to fight for King Charles I. The former Llanrhos schoolroom, opposite the church, was built in 1822 by Frances Mostyn, then aged 73, of Bodysgallen, and closed about a century ago.

One of the more pathetic tombstones in the churchyard is inscribed: "Here lyeth the body of poor Betty, who for upwards of 50 years was [a] houseless wandering maniac, died Feb 1824. Y mae gorphwysfa yn a Nefoedd." (i.e. "she rests in heaven").

Passing over the brow of the hill, on the way to Conwy, one passes Tŷ'n-y-coed, built in 1878 for a Liverpool timber merchant. It was bought in 1891 by Birmingham Hospital Saturday Fund, and opened in 1892 as their first convalescent home. In 1971 it was converted into the Harriet Robertson Research Institute, specialising in international geological exploration.

Beyond, and now cut off by Wormhout Way, is Marl Hall. It was seriously damaged by fire in 1730 and there was a mature tree growing out of the entrance hall when Birmingham Hospital Saturday Fund bought it in 1894. It was 1903 before the house was restored and ready for occupation by 80 women. It was again sold in 1967 for use as a privately run nursing home, and again in 1971 (for £24,000) to Warwickshire Council for use as field study centre.

The parish of Llanrhos was formally absorbed within the Llandudno Urban District (together with Glanwydden, Penrhyn Bay, Penrhynside, Pydew and Llangystennin) by virtue of the Caernarvonshire Review Order, 1935. Llandudno Urban District was, in turn, absorbed within Aberconwy Borough of the new county of Gwynedd, as part of the reorganisation of local government in Wales, in April 1974. There was yet another reorganization of local government in 1996 when Llandudno became part of the new County Borough of Conwy.

Three Llandudno veterans of the Wormhout ambush at the unveiling of one of the two memorials to the prisoners massacred at Esquelbecq, on the orders of SS officer Wilhelm Mohnke, after being captured in the River Peene Becque.

WORMHOUT WAY 13

Wormhout Way has boundary notices at either end to tell travellers Llandudno is twinned with the little French town where the local Territorial Army regiment was ambushed in 1940 by the SS *Regiment Leibstandarte Adolf Hitler*, led by the notorious Wilhelm Mohnke. There are matching roadside notices on the boundaries of Wormhout saying: *"Jumelée avec Llandudno, Pays de Galles"* – although displaying the Union flag rather than the Red Dragon of Pays de Galles!

Wormhout is a town of 5,000 people, ten miles from Dunkerque, on the Lille road. Its citizens proudly proclaim themselves to be Flemish, living in the Flemish Houtland, but their only language is now French – in the same way as Llandudno's citizens are proud of being Welsh though most of them can now speak only in English. Wormhout's central feature is the market square, with its tall war memorial surmounted by a bronze statue of a French soldier of World War One. It stands outside the Town Hall. The tree-lined square also has a popular and much-used bandstand. St. Martin's church, in the square, became famous on 25 April 1406 as the scene of a miracle when its statue of the Virgin was seen to weep. The three-nave church is well endowed with Baroque furnishings and some 17th century paintings.

As the inevitability of war became apparent in 1939 the Territorial Army of part-time volunteers was doubled by dividing existing units into two, with each half then recruiting to full strength. Thus the 69th Medium Regiment (Caernarvon & Denbigh Yeomanry) was born on 1 July 1939, out of the older 61st Medium Regiment.

Commanded by Lieut-Colonel C.B. Arnold, DSO, and with its headquarters at Llandudno Drill Hall, in Argyll Road, the new regiment absorbed 241 and 242 Batteries, comprising A Troop (Bangor), B Troop (Anglesey), C Troop (Caernarfon) and D Troop (Llandudno). The new regiment was mobilised on 1 September 1939 and posted to billets at St. Asaph, where the Plough Hotel became the other ranks mess hall. In November they moved to Chipping Sodbury, near Bristol, where their obsolete 6 inch (15cm) howitzers were replaced by 4.5 inch (11cm) gun-howitzers. Lieut-Col. Arnold left to command a training regiment and Lieut-Col. John D'Arcy became Commanding Officer.

In the first week of May 1940 the regiment landed at Le Havre, and marched until nightfall to a château near Coutrai, in Belgium. Next morning they moved up into the line, passing retreating Belgian troops who gave the demoralised thumbs-down sign. Later that morning they were preparing their guns for action when they lost their first man, Gunner Kitchener Jones "Yr Ogof," killed by a German shell. Although in a well-camouflaged position, the 69th were being circled by an enemy spotter plane, and were subjected to accurate enemy artillery fire. Only when leaving did they discover that a local farmer had, by pure mischance, cut his corn in the shape of a V pointing directly to them.

The regiment remained in action continuously, firing by day and moving by night, their last gun position being at Mont Kemmel. There they were ordered to spike their guns and they reluctantly rammed shells down both ends of their barrels, ran out 100 yard (91m) lanyards, and fired for the last time, to see the barrels split open. Personal weapons were not then on general issue to all gunners, and it was with only a handful of rifles and revolvers that they set out for Dunkerque.

The 69th soon found themselves snarled up with countless thousands of troops and civilians, all trying to escape, and Captain the Earl of Aylesford, commanding Llandudno's D Troop, decided to take a short-cut, via Wormhout, which he thought was being defended by the Royal Warwickshire Regiment. Unwittingly he led them into an ambush laid in the town by the German SS.

Lord Aylesford died when a light shell hit his truck as they crossed the little River Peene Becque, a few yards from the Market Square, to signal the start of concentrated small arms fire from hidden enemy positions. Several men were killed or wounded and the rest scrambled down into the river. Just then it began to rain heavily, reducing visibility for the German snipers. About 35 men who went downriver eventually reached Dunkerque, where some were killed and others were among the last to leave the beach, aboard the Isle of Man Steam Packet Company's ship *Tynwald*.

The gunners who waded upstream were killed or captured. The Llandudno prisoners were grouped with men of the Cheshire and Royal Warwickshire Regiments captured at nearby Esquelbecq, nearer to Dunkerque. All were marched to a barn, those who could not keep up being prodded with bayonets or shot. They had fallen into the hands of No.5 Coy, of the 2nd Battalion of the most ruthless of the SS regiments, the *Leibstandarte Adolf Hitler* – raised in 1928 from Nazi fanatics chosen to create Hitler's personal bodyguard. Seventy men of Llandudno's D Troop were killed or wounded.

Scene of the 1940 ambush of Llandudno's Territorial Army volunteers by the SS Regiment Leibstandarte Adolf Hitler.

With one exception, the wounded and other prisoners of Wormhout never came home. Five stick grenades were hurled into the barn, which the SS then entered to shoot any prisoners who were still alive. Gunner Tudor Parry, of Llandudno, had been partially blown through a gap in the wall, and on trying to pick himself up he saw an SS trooper raise his rifle and shoot him in the face.

Two days later a burial party of Austrian soldiers came to the barn to remove about 90 bodies and, on finding Gnr. Parry still alive took him to a field hospital manned by captured men of the Royal Army Medical Corps, including Llandudno pharmacist Eric Fernhead. Staff-Sergeant Fernhead recognised Parry, nursed him back to health, and $3^1/_2$ years later escorted him home to Llandudno in a Red Cross exchange of permanently disabled prisoners. Only then did the world learn of the massacre in the barn at Esquelbecq.

In 1945 British Intelligence discovered that the acting battalion commander at Wormhout and Esquelbecq was SS-Haupsturmführer Wilhelm Mohnke, aged 29, who ended the war as Brigadeführer, commanding the SS at Hitler's Chancellery in Berlin. The equally notorious Josef "Sepp" Dietrich, CO of *Leibstandarte Adolf Hitler* in 1940, told British investigators he had been wounded on the road to Wormhout when his truck was hit by an anti-tank round – fired by Pte. Harry Cookson, of the 2nd Royal Warwickshires. He said he was sheltering in a ditch during the atrocity and that with both himself and his second-in-command out of action Haupsturmführer Mohnke assumed command of the battalion – which remained an independent elite unit of the SS throughout the war. (In 1946 an Allied court sentenced Dietrich to 25 years imprisonment for other war crimes. Released after 10 years, he was arrested by the Germans and sentenced to 19 months for his role in the 1934 Nazi purge of its own ranks known as the Night of the Long Knives).

Mohnke was born at Lübeck in May 1911 and volunteered for Hitler's bodyguard in 1935. Canadian investigators identified him as the man responsible for the execution of about 130 of their prisoners in Normandy, in 1944. American investigators uncovered a similar execution of between 72 and 86 of their prisoners at Malmedy, together with 600 Belgians. The Greek Government put Mohnke on their list of criminals wanted for war atrocities throughout the Balkans. However Mohnke appeared to have vanished in 1945. Unknown to the Western Allies he was captured by the Russians after fleeing from the Chancellery, where he was the last to see Hitler alive before he killed himself, and then supervised the burning of Hitler's body. Without informing the Western Allies, the Soviets took him to the Lubyanka Prison, in Moscow, for interrogation. He was quietly released ten years later and promptly awarded a major-general's pension by the West German government.

Under pressure from Britain the public prosecutor at Lübeck opened a file on Mohnke in 1988 but closed it in 1994, saying there was insufficient evidence on which to prosecute. The Americans have never replied to an allegation that Mohnke was protected by a CIA deal, in exchange for detailing what he had observed in the Lubyanka, and cooperating in investigations about his senior SS comrades who had merged into influential positions in post-war Germany and Austria. The British Army's twenty-two files of their own 1945-46 investigation are inscribed: "The murder of a considerable number of British prisoners-of-war by members of the German armed forces at Wormhoudt, France, on 28th May 1940," and were made available to the public in 1994, at which time General Mohnke was living 15 miles from Hamburg on a £22,000 a year pension. British investigators had an affidavit from SS-Private Heinz Schmidt saying Mohnke ordered the shooting of the Wormhout prisoners. SS-Corporal Oskar Senf said Untersturmführer (second-lieutenant) Heinrich was reprimanded by Mohnke for taking prisoners, and was ordered to dispose of them. Only one officer (Obersturmführer Karl Kummert) made a signed statement saying Mohnke ordered the elimination of the prisoners at

The town twinning sign at the entrance to Wormhout, in Flanders. Llandudno ex-Servicemen are seen parading their standards at Wormhout parish church. Below are some of the War Graves Commission headstones in Wormhout cemetery, including those of the Llandudno troop commander, Captain the Earl of Aylesford and L/Bdr. J.Coleman.

4pm that day, but the file shows the events were precisely as described by Gunner Parry.

In 1973 the Dunkirk Veterans Association erected a prominent inscribed stone beside the road linking Esquelbecq and Wormhout, commemorating the 1940 massacre. In September 1988 the mayor of Wormhout, former Resistance soldier Robert Deldicque, led a delegation to Llandudno to sign a twinning agreement between the two towns, and on 14 April 1989 the Mayor of Llandudno, Tom White, led a reciprocal deputation to Wormhout – after which the commemorative boundary signs were unveiled jointly by the two mayors. On 3 November 1996 Llandudno Town Council consolidated the twinning with inscribed tablets of Llechwedd slate, set in a red brick plinth, unveiled by the Mayor, Mike Hold, near the bleak site of the barn. The plaques state (in French and English): "Here the Esquelbecq massacre took place, 28th May 1940." While Canon Philip Cousins, Rector of Llandudno, was dedicating the memorial a French cyclist arrived to tell the assembled Llandudno veterans that Mohnke had just died at his Hamburg home, aged 85, after his second heart attack.

Robert Deldicque, who was Mayor of Wormhout from 1977 to 1995, commented: "He was never interrogated by the Germans or the Western Allies." It was M. Deldicque's research that identified the twenty scattered graves of the British soldiers, including men of the 69th Regiment, who were re-interred in 1941 by the citizens of Wormhout, and are now marked by Commonwealth War Graves Commission headstones in the town cemetery.

"The public prosecutor at Lubeck confirmed to us that he had not so much as invited Mohnke to his office, saying there was no likelihood of his coming in to make a confession. And now this criminal has died in his bed," added M. Deldicque.

Ironically, the war of the 69th Medium Regiment was destined to end at Dunkerque – but not in 1940. The survivors were first re-equipped as coastal defence artillery on the South Coast, where they lost seven men in the bombing of Ford Naval Air Station on 18 August 1940, at the height of the Battle of Britain. On 28 July 1942 they boarded the troop ship *Samaria*, at Liverpool, for the long voyage around the southern tip of Africa, and disembarked at Port Suez, Egypt, on 21 September. After calibrating their 4.5 and 5.5-inch gun howitzers, at Almaza, near Cairo, they moved into the front line two miles south of El Alamein. At 9.40pm on 23 October the 69th Medium Regiment was ordered to fire 300 rounds per gun, as part of the famous barrage which dislodged the *Afrika Korps*. Thereafter the 69th fought the Germans right across North Africa. Christmas Day found them on the borders of Tripolitania; by St. David's Day 1943 they were trying to clear the *Afrika Korps* out of Tunis.

From Tunisia the gunners put to sea in landing craft for a very long and uncomfortable voyage to take part in the invasion of Salerno on 9 September 1943. They fought with the 5th Army until the capture of Monte Casino, on 17 May 1944, after which they were taken to Palestine for re-equipping with new guns. Then it was back to Taranto, to rejoin the 8th Army, with whom they fought their last Italian battle on 19 December 1944.

The 69th Medium Regiment was next sent to Marseilles, and moved up through France to have the satisfaction of being instrumental in driving the Germans out of Dunkerque in 1945. They had come full circle in five years, and were still at Dunkerque when the war in Europe ended.

The great and the good of Europe were photographed by Thomas Edge in his studio at the junction of Gloddaeth Street and Bodhyfryd Road. The Astra cinema is seen below after it had closed in 1987. Formerly the Winter Gardens, and then the Odeon, it was once Wales's biggest opera house. Anne Edwards (inset) was the only Caernarvonshire principal soprano to sing in her home county with both the Royal Carl Rosa Opera and Welsh National Opera.

Commencing at the memorial to the dead of World Wars One & Two, in Prince Edward Square, the narrowest section of the Llandudno isthmus is traversed in a straight line via Gloddaeth Street and Gloddaeth Avenue – a mere 1,380 yards (1262m) from shore to shore. With the national classification of roads in 1936 Prince Edward Square became the start of the A496 Llandudno-Fishguard trunk road, a distinction it retained until the re-numbering of the North-South routes in 1972. On the earliest known map of Llandudno, prepared in 1742 by Thomas Badeslade, surveyor to Sir Thomas Mostyn, a network of ditches and streams drained into Y *Ffos Fawr* (meaning "the big ditch") which joined the sea near the present war memorial.

Prince Edward Square was the site of the Gorsedd circle erected for the 1864 National Eisteddfod. Matthew Arnold has left us a description of the scene: "The presiding genius of the mystic circle, in our hideous nineteenth-century costume relieved only by a green scarf, the wind drowning his voice and the dust powdering his whiskers, looked thoroughly wretched; so did the aspirants for bardic honours; and I believe, after about an hour of it, we all of us, as we stood shivering round the sacred stones, began half to wish for the Druid's sacrificial knife to end our sufferings." Clwydfardd (David Griffith) and Gwalchmai (Rev. Richard Parry) appear to have shared the duties of Archdruid at the 1864 Eisteddfod.

After crossing Mostyn Street into Gloddaeth Street let us commence our tour on the north (Great Orme) side. Marie et Cie, the ladies outfitters occupying Nos. 2, 4 & 6, used to have a board over the main entrance proclaiming: "By appointment to Her Majesty the Queen of Roumania," – another reminder of the 1890 visit. Far more exciting were the visits to the shop of Nina Scott, in 1968, and Lynda Goldstraw in 1970, two girls judged to have the loveliest legs in Great Britain in their respective years. Nos. 4 & 6 were added to the shop in the 1920s, having served the town for many years as a Post Office, in which role the electric telegraph was installed in 1869.

The low building next door, now a newsagent's, was built as the photographic studio of Thomas Edge, whose daughters married into the town's most influential families. Originally from Fylde, he began life as a seaman but later set up a studio in Preston, before moving to Llandudno in 1862. He soon attracted everyone of note to his studio, and there are surviving prints of Dean Liddell, and of his daughters Alice and Lorina. Edge's wife Jeannie Catherine managed the studio and an adjoining art shop, next door to what became Marie et Cie. They had four daughters, one of whom (Elsie May) married James Jones Marks, County Court Registrar and chairman of Llandudno Urban Council 1906-07. Another (Kate) married Mostyn Estate Agent and architect G.A. Humphreys. A third Edge daughter married the brother of G.A. Humphreys. Thomas Edge's son Frank became editor of the *Llandudno Advertiser*. Elsie May Marks was the grandmother of Brigadier J.M. Herbert-Roberts (mentioned in Chapter 5, Church Walks).

Clarence Hotel occupies the site of the town's first Presbyterian chapel, built in 1813. During World War Two the One Ash Hotel, at 20 Gloddaeth Street, was requisitioned to serve as headquarters for the Coast Artillery School, staffed mostly by the ATS (Auxiliary Territorial Service, forerunner of the Women's Royal Army Corps which was disbanded in 1992). In 1940 it was visited by the Princess Royal (Victoria Alexandra Alice Mary), wearing ATS uniform. She was the sister of King George VI.

In Clement Avenue, the Risboro Hotel was built in 1887 as W. A. Whiston's Collegiate School for Boys, offering: "Preparation for commercial life, also for London university, local preceptors and professional examinations. Special technical courses for engineering, architecture, building, etc." It was for sale, as a going concern, in November 1895 when the local intermediate education governors were looking for premises for a rate-aided secondary school. After rejecting Drummond Villa, the Carlton Hotel, the English Baptist and Congregational schoolrooms, the governors bought Mr. Whiston'a school, complete with furniture and fifty fee-paying pupils, for £567. This was the start of John Bright School, concerning which we will read a little more in Chapter 17 (Vaughan Street area).

Eagle or albatross? After 31 years of barrack-room controversy about the bird depicted in the Royal Air Force badge an Air Ministry order was issued in 1949 declaring it to be an eagle. Alas the Air Ministry was wrong for the badge was designed by Charles L. Pepper, who lived at The Gables, in Gloddaeth Avenue, and whose model was a stuffed albatross at the British Museum. "I rejected the eagle because it was the badge of the Germans who were then our enemy," Mr. Pepper told the author. As an architect he was drafted into the Royal Naval Air Service seaplane drawing room, at the Cecil Hotel, in The Strand. "We were asked to design a badge for the new RAF in 1918 and I got landed with the job," he reminisced. As Chief Petty Officer Pepper his only reward was a letter of thanks from Sir William Weir, the then Air Minister, together with instructions to design the official seal of the RAF – a letter which Mr. Pepper cherished for the rest of his life.

To explore the opposite side of Gloddaeth Street we return to the roundabout at the intersection with Mostyn Street. Winson House, at No.1, is interesting as the boarding house above the jeweller's shop of George Lowe, where Viscountess Newry stayed during the summer of 1862 – the summer in which she was involved in an Oxford quarrel with Lewis Carroll. Her fellow guests included the Very Reverend Thomas Woodward, Dean of Down, Ireland, with his wife and sister-in-law. Also present were three of her daughters and a son – but not her 20-years-old son, Francis Charles, Lord Newry, a student at Christ Church.

The Palladium Theatre was built in 1920 with 1,500 seats in three tiers. It replaced a market hall built in 1864 by the Llandudno Market Hall Company (formed in 1862). Between the two world wars it had an orchestra of twelve and offered a blend of drama, variety, musical comedy and ballet, its stars including Gracie Fields and Harry Korris. It had been a bingo hall for about a decade when, in 1972, a ceiling was placed over the stalls to retain bingo on the ground floor with a 600-seat cinema above. During 2000-01 the Palladium was converted into a Wetherspoons pub but many of the interior features, including the balcony and its seating, have had to be retained because of its "listed building" status. Garden Street, beside the theatre, leads to the rival market hall built by the Urban Council in 1897.

London society hairdresser André Bernard opened a salon at No. 9 Gloddaeth Street in 1969. A year later he was found dead, with two bullets in the back of the head, in his open-topped sports car in Hyde Park. The murderer was never found.

Chapel Street (originally Pony Street) takes its name from the English Presbyterian church at the corner with Gloddaeth Street. The cause began in 1879 with services at the Masonic Hall. A corrugated-iron chapel was built on the present site in 1880, the schoolroom was added in 1886, and the original chapel was replaced by the present building in 1891.

For 55 years the dominant building in Gloddaeth Street was its 1,983-seat cinema. It was built as the Winter Gardens Cinema Theatre and Ballroom in 1934, on the site of The Vineyard, a walled market garden noted for its fruit. It was built by Rochdale brothers James and Zachry Brierley, who had settled in Llandudno in 1920 as motor-coach operators. Their £70,000 entertainment centre was opened by male impersonator Ella Shields, with a telephone message relayed by loud-speaker from Gracie Fields. The cinema part of the enterprise was soon taken over by the Odeon company, who installed a Christie theatre organ built by Hill, which was inaugurated on 25 March 1935 by Harold Ramsay.

Carl Rosa Opera returned to Llandudno in August 1955, after an absence of 55 years, and brought with them Caernarfon soprano Anne Edwards. Ignoring all the town's recognised theatres they went to the Odeon Cinema, which proved to be a popular venue for a season of *La Bohème, Rigoletto, Cav & Pag, Faust, the Barber of Seville,* and *Il Trovatore.* By June of the following year Anne Edwards was the Carl Rosa's Mimi for their season at Sadler's Wells.

After their Festival of Britain season at the Grand Theatre in 1951 the Welsh National Opera had no plans to return to Llandudno, the original Victorian and Edwardian operatic centre of North Wales. The author consistently campaigned for the company's return, notably in the columns of the *Daily Post* and by frequently calling to see WNO founder W.H. Smith in Cardiff. He was aided and abetted by Mr. Smith's secretary Margaret Moreland (who later became a member of the WNO Board), and by Llandudno Odeon manager Roy Bentley. For their week's season at Llandudno in August 1957 the WNO engaged Anne Edwards, who had sung Marguerite in their highly acclaimed revival of Boito's forgotten *Mefistofele,* at Sadler's Wells, in the June. She was given parts in the opening performance of *Nabucco* (Verdi's 1842 masterpiece which the WNO had rescued from obscurity in 1952) and for the closing performance of *I Lombardi,* giving her the distinction of being the only Caernarvonshire singer to appear in her home county with both the original Carl Rosa company and the Welsh National Opera. From Llandudno she went on to Sadler's Wells and the Royal Opera House, Covent Garden, and to such heights as the lead soprano for the Shah of Iran's opening of the Teheran Opera House (Rudaki Hall) with a performance of *Nabucco.*

During the WNO years the Odeon became an opera house with an international reputation, and was the biggest theatre in Wales after the closure of the Capitol Cinema, in Cardiff, in the 1970s. The seating capacity was reduced to 1,643 in 1957, to provide space for an opera orchestra, and until the opening of the small 540-seat Theatr Clwyd, in Mold, the Llandudno Odeon was the only North Wales theatre with a stage and flies capable of accommodating the full range of grand opera. The WNO season grew from one to two weeks, attracting singers of the stature of Gwyneth Jones, who happily commuted between Bayreuth (Wagner's Bavarian home) and Llandudno. In 1968 American mezzo-soprano Joy Davidson made her British debut at Llandudno, in the role of Carmen. There was an amusing incident in 1978 when the WNO publicity officer discovered that Llandudno's visitors were staying away from the theatre because they believed the Welsh National Opera sang in the Welsh language. He scurried about the town amending the posters for *The Marriage of Figaro, La Bohème, The Barber of Seville, Il Trovatore,* and *A Midsummer Night's Dream* with stickers proclaiming: "All operas sung in English." Those were the days before the current elitist fashion of singing everything in the original language. Sadler's Wells Ballet appeared at the Odeon theatre in 1955, and the D'Oyly Carte Opera, who had last appeared at Llandudno in 1907, returned in 1971 and 1972, with the famous John Reed heading the singers on both occasions, and were back again in 1980. The Rank Organisation sold the Odeon to Alan Hutchinson's Astra chain in 1969, from when it became known as the Astra Theatre. Alan Hutchinson died in 1984 and the theatre again changed hands in the following year. It closed in 1986 and was demolished in 1989 to be replaced by the present block of flats.

Beyond the Astra the road was known as Green Lane when opened by Reginald Cust in the 1860s. It was along this lane that Llandudno & Colwyn Bay Electric Railway Ltd. laid their 3 ft 6 ins (1.07m) gauge tram track in 1907, with an ambitious plan (never carried out) for extending the tram service to Deganwy at one end and Prestatyn at the other. By the time the last tram set out from the West Shore terminus on 24 March 1956 the line had carried 130,000,000 passengers.

A watercolour by Dean Henry G. Liddell, father of Alice of Wonderland fame, showing Penmorfa, the house he had built on the West Shore in 1862, and which was subsequently extended to form the Gogarth Abbey Hotel, as seen in the 1934 photograph – which also shows the 19th century miners' cottages.

WEST SHORE

15

Strikingly different from the more popular northern promenade, on the opposite side of the Llandudno isthmus, the West Shore was Alice Liddell's true Wonderland for eleven years of her childhood and teenage Christmas, Easter and summer holidays. The romance of the West Shore, or Penmorfa, began in 1284 when Edward I presented the land to the Bishop of Bangor as a gift for christening the first English Prince of Wales (claimed to have been born at Caernarfon although the evidence points to Rhuddlan Castle). When the Bishop's lands were surveyed in 1680 it was found that the Mostyn family had enclosed so many random plots that the boundaries were "so utterly broke up and destroyed that it is impossible to find them out." Boundaries had become important with the re-discovery of copper in the bowels of the Great Orme, and it was in conjunction with the copper mines that a dozen cottages were built on the West Shore sand dunes in 1783. A terrace of them, running at right angles to the sea, stood across the southern gable of the Gogarth Abbey Hotel until 1936.

One of the old cottages survives incongruously, at the end of Abbey Place, a cul-de-sac with an interesting walled channel through which a constant river flows out of the mountain (and into the model yacht pond built in 1896). The river emerges through the stone lined exit of an 874 yards (799m) long adit, or drainage tunnel, from the New Mine. It was completed in 1842, after eight years and eight months of continuous excavation by a team of twelve miners, who worked in shifts, night and day. Rails were laid through this tunnel to bring the ore out of the mine for crushing and separation, and loading into small vessels beached on receding tides. In 1997 contractors spent six weeks lining the tunnel with pipes to ensure constant drainage and prevent the accumulation of water within the mountain due to hidden rock falls – water that would eventually force its way out somewhere.

It was here that Llandudno's short-lived shipbuilding industry produced but one vessel, the 34-ton sloop *Sarah Lloyd*, launched in 1863. She was named after the wife of Captain David Lloyd who gave up the sea in 1861 to take out the last lease of the Llandudno mines. His 1862 output (from the Old Mine) was 1,300 tons but in the following year it slumped to a miserable 104. Instead of carrying a copper fortune to the smelters the *Sarah Lloyd* earned her keep as a coastal tramp, until wrecked at Aberdaron in 1874. Captain Lloyd died in 1875 and although a little ore was still being mined two years later Mrs. Lloyd finally surrendered the lease in 1881, thus ending Llandudno's copper story. Their son John was lost overboard off the Cape of Good Hope, on passage from Madras in 1861, aged 19.

Into this decadent setting walked the Very Reverend Henry Liddell, 50-years-old Dean of Christ Church, Oxford, during his 1861 Easter vacation, which as noted in Chapter 9 (North Parade and Happy Valley), was spent at Llandudno. Shrewdly anticipating the demise of the industrial activity, in what was otherwise a peaceful rabbit warren, he went to the Mostyn Estate office and leased a building plot in the middle of it all.

A mock gothic four-storey house, built mostly of red and white glazed bricks brought all the way from Ruabon, was soon rising on the site although the work stopped early in 1862 because of some dispute that led the Dean to dismiss his local contractor. In April the task of completion was given to a Caernarfon builder who immediately put forty men on the job, under the supervision of his son. Contrary to what has been written by the Dean's biographer, the Reverend H. L. Thompson (and all who have relied upon Thompson), subsequent progress was rapid. On 16 August 1862 a delighted Dean Liddell gave the contractor and his men a supper of roast beef, plum pudding and beer to celebrate the completion, and called his house *Penmorfa*. He made a short speech to which the men responded by endorsing the toast of their chairman, contractor Robert Williams: "The health of the Very Reverend Dean and his family, and long life and happiness to them."

A few days later the children and their governess were photographed on the steps of the house, with the still unfinished garden in the foreground. This photograph, and another taken from Monks' Path showing part of the house, is preserved in an album that Lewis Carroll gave to Alice at the end of 1862. Carroll was meticulous in cataloguing his negatives and there is no mention of these pictures. He may have bought the print from Llandudno photographer Thomas Edge, or Alice could have added it later, for the same album contains a photograph of the Dean and Mrs. Liddell taken in 1866 at Penrhyn Castle, by Georgiana Berkeley (showing also the resident Douglas-Pennant family, Bishop and Mrs. Wilberforce, Mrs. W.E. Gladstone, and others).

Penmorfa has remained virtually intact and is readily identifiable within what has grown into the present Gogarth Abbey Hotel – which is an amalgamation of five distinct properties. When viewed from the front, the hotel has a low extension wing on the left. This is the dining room added in 1936. Next comes the Dean's house, to which there was originally a central entrance at first floor level, now replaced by a window. The third section, of mock-Elizabethan timbered appearance, is a 1920s link to what was once a pair of semi-detached houses called Belorme and Berthddu.

Letters written from Penmorfa tell us the house was used regularly for very long Easter, summer and Christmas vacations. The Liddells hosted many distinguished visitors to Llandudno, including William Gladstone, Matthew Arnold (Professor of Poetry at Oxford), Sir Henry Acland, Samuel Wilberforce (Bishop of Oxford), Sir Charles Newton (Keeper of Greek and Roman Antiquities at the British Museum) and his artist wife Mary.

Although the Dean would return early to Oxford, his family seemed to enjoy very long Christmas holidays, as we see from a birthday letter which Alice wrote to her father from Penmorfa on 5 February 1863: "Yesterday we had another gale ... Edith and I had our bed moved down into Harry's room, we lay on two mattresses on the floor and were very comfortable indeed. Little Rhoda had her little cot down into Mama's room, where Pickey [i.e. governess Mary Prickett] and Ina slept, and Mama was in the Blue Room, altogether we were very jolly." At that time Edith was aged nearly 9, Alice nearly 11, Harry 16, Rhoda nearly 4, and Ina [Lorina] was nearly 14. A sketch preserved among Alice's papers detailed how the rooms were occupied – her room was at the rear on the top floor, and is now obscured by later extensions to the building. There were drawing rooms to the left and the right of the main entrance hall; the Dean slept immediately above the front door and Mrs. Liddell had the bedroom to the right; Lorina slept in the room above the Dean; Harry's room was at the rear, at the same level as the front entrance; the Governess slept in a room next to Alice, and there were two nurseries at the same level.

[Sir] William Richmond, then only 21, spent eight weeks at Penmorfa in 1864, to paint his famous study *The Sisters*, portraying Alice, Edith and Lorina, against a backdrop of the Great Orme. The girls sat in the large third-storey room to the left of the house when viewed from the front, behind which was the family schoolroom. The Great Orme was later painted in, with almost photographic accuracy, from a window in the schoolroom. The picture was hung the following April at the Royal Institution.

In April 1872 Mrs. Liddell wrote to Alice, on holiday in the Mediterranean as part of the traditional Grand Tour of Europe: "Mr. Taylor has written to offer £2,000 for Penmorfa – we have taken time to consider. Poor Penmorfa! Well, we all had some happy days there." The house was sold in 1873 to the Reverend Robert Taylor, Vicar of Warthill, near York, in anticipation of his retirement at the end of the following year.

The Liddells may not have used their Llandudno home after 1871 – or did they? Queen Victoria's youngest son Prince Leopold secretly visited Llandudno in August 1873, staying incognito at the Imperial Hotel, with his loyal ADC, temporary major-general John Patten. Why did he seek out Llandudno, and why in this fashion? Leopold matriculated to Christ Church in 1872, and was frequently entertained by the Liddells at the Deanery, which forms an integral part of the college buildings. He was a year younger than Alice and there was said to be obvious affection between them – and perhaps an ambitious desire on the part of Mrs. Liddell to marry one of her daughters into the Royal Family. We know from a note in Alice's hand, written when she was 80, and which remained with the family until the 2001 auction of her memorabilia, that there was at least one occasion when Leopold took Alice for a boat ride on the river in Oxford. Any romance between them would have peaked in 1873, but would soon have been suppressed. Could Alice, then aged 21, have visited Penmorfa for the last time in that August of 1873, for a secret tryst with Leopold? When she married in 1880 she received a letter from the prince, sending his "warmest and most heart-felt wishes for your future happiness," and adding: "I shall think much of you and your family tomorrow; for you know how I have felt and sympathised with you and yours, in your joys and your sorrows." Two years later Prince Leopold married Princess Helene of Waldeck. When Alice's second son was born in January 1883, she named him Leopold. When Prince leopold's daughter was born a few weeks later she was named Alice (the future Countess of Athlone).

The ugly building pretending to be a promenade shelter, in front of the Gogarth Abbey Hotel, is a sewerage pumping station control room, with stand-by generator. It was approved by the local planning authority as Welsh Water's simplistic solution to problems caused in 1993, when exceptional rainfall put the 1992 replacement for 1970 underground equipment out of action, and worsened the flooding in the town. The town's first sewers were installed in 1857 and still service most of the older part of the town. In August 1865 Dean Liddell protested to the Improvement Commissioners about the dreadful stench from the outfall pipe in front of his house. The best solution Medical Officer Dr. James Nicol could recommend was the insertion of ventilating boxes loaded with charcoal, and the stench persisted intermittently until 1895, when the outfall was extended. Now all sewage is treated before discharge on the ebb tide.

There are enormous underground storage tanks stretching from the pumping station to the model yacht pond, with two stovepipe ventilators disguised to look like ornate street lamps – and from which there is an occasional unpleasant whiff.

Here one finds the town's Lewis Carroll memorial, usually known as the White Rabbit statue, and towards which every child in Llandudno donated a penny. It is inscribed: "On this very shore, during happy rambles with Alice Liddell, LEWIS CARROLL was inspired to write that literary treasure *Alice in Wonderland,* which has charmed children for generations. Unveiled by the Rt. Hon. David Lloyd George, OM, MP, September 6th, 1933."

Unfortunately for Llandudno there is not the slightest doubt that Carroll's inspiration came when he first told the story during a boat ride on the River Isis (the Oxford section of the Thames) on 4 July 1862. He completed his manuscript by 10 February 1863 and his illustrations were completed by 13 September 1864.

Neither is there any evidence that Lewis Carroll, the pen name of the Reverend Charles Lutwidge Dodgson, ever visited Llandudno. To be meaningful in relation to his writing of *Alice's Adventures Under Ground* any such visit would have to have taken place during 1862-

Angela Hazeldine (left), in Alice costume beside Llandudno's Lewis Carroll memorial in 1988, is now a Channel 5 TV presenter. The original hallway of Penmorfa retains the stairs used by Alice Liddell at her Llandudno Wonderland. In the picture below David Lloyd George is seen unveiling the White Rabbit statue in 1933.

64. In his diary for 8 August 1862 he wrote: "In the morning happened to cross the quad-rangle as the two flies from the Deanery were driving out, and so got a last sight of my young friends." The Liddells were on their way to Llandudno for their first summer at Penmorfa. Carroll makes no mention of the family after that until 28 October, when he noted: "Called on Mrs. Liddell, to ask leave for the artist at Shrimpton's, who is going to colour my photo-graphs of the children, to call and have a sitting, so as to get good likenesses. She simply evaded the question. (I have been out of her good books ever since Lord Newry's business)." He had already noted on 25 May a problem relating to college rules for a ball that under-graduate Lord Newry wanted to arrange. The 20-years-old heir to Viscount Newry was very friendly with Mrs. Liddell, and Carroll noted: "I am afraid much ill-feeling will result." Lord Newry's mother was also on holiday at Llandudno during that summer of 1862. All that would seem to rule out the remotest chance of the humble stuttering deacon being invited to the Dean's house at Penmorfa that summer. Neither is it likely that he would have forgotten to mention such a visit in his diary. In the following year Carroll noted on 30 June: "The Dean-ery party left for Llandudno," and his next mention of them is not until 16 October: "Met the Liddells." There is nothing of significance to Llandudno in the 1864 diary.

Alice, then Mrs. Hargreaves, aged 84, and living in Kent, was invited to the 1933 unveiling of the White Rabbit statue but apologised for her inability to attend, writing: "Increasing age makes physical adventures in Wonderland more and more difficult to achieve. I still have the happiest memories of Penmorfa, as my father's house at Llandudno was then called, and of the rambles over the Great Orme's Head and among the Llandudno sand hills. I wish I could come personally in gratitude for those joyous days, and for the days spent with Mr. Dodgson."

In the nearby Church of Our Saviour there is a lesser-known plaque stating: "This tablet records the fact that the font in this church was the gift of children in memory of Lewis Carroll (C. L. Dodgson), the author of *Alice in Wonderland,* and a lover of Llandudno." The font was dedicated by Bishop Watkin Williams, of Bangor (a former student of Dodgson), on 30 July 1912, the day on which the church was consecrated. (The plaque misspells Carroll's name).

Much of today's local government confusion about Carroll, with the wish being father to the thought, stems from misinformation written in the *Llandudno Advertiser* at the time of his death on 14 January 1898, such as: "Many residents of Llandudno will remember Lewis Carroll who was for many years a visitor to this town." It went on to claim that Carroll wrote *Alice Adventures in Wonderland* at Llandudno. The local paper was equally confused when Dean Liddell died four days later, saying he was a constant visitor for a quarter of a century, and adding that Carroll composed his *Wonderland* to amuse Alice while she was ill at Penmorfa in 1865.

The Church in Wales is now in the process of selling the Church of Our Saviour in Septem-ber 2002, to Zion English Baptist Church, who have been using a former bank in Craig-y-don after losing their original Mostyn Street chapel in 1967. The intending new owners have un-dertaken to preserve the Lewis Carroll memorial font. A less obvious memorial in the Church of Our Saviour is a window of 16th century Spanish glass from the Netherlands, now deprived of its natural light by structural extensions on the south side. It was given by Sir Thomas Hughes Neave, the 5th baronet, of Llysdulas, near Amlwch, in memory of his brother and heir, Major Arundell Neave, who was killed at Ypres on 21 February 1915, while serving with the 16th Queen's Lancers.

A car park, between the church and the sea, gives access to all that is left of the West Shore sand dunes, where Charles Darwin killed a viper in 1824. (Darwin's niece, Anne Eliza Thomasine Darwin, died at Llandudno in July 1904, aged 76). Beneath the car park, low tides expose the rotting keel of the *Flying Foam,* a Bridgewater schooner wrecked in 1936 while carrying a cargo of coal. The shoreline between the car park and the Great Orme is protected by an unusually deep sea wall, 2,885 feet (879m) long, completed in 1952. Landward of the sea wall there is a flood barrier built in 1936, and thrice since overtopped by storm-lashed waves that have surged up Gloddaeth Avenue. In 1991 the sea defences on the West Shore were reinforced with modern barriers made of enormous loose boulders – delivered by heavy trucks making 105 trips a day for several weeks.

The sand dunes lead to the North Wales Golf Club, first laid out in 1893 as a 9-hole course, with its original clubhouse on the site of the present West Shore Garage, at the corner of Herkomer Road. It was subsequently extended to the present 18 holes with such challenging names as the Sahara (8th), Hades (13th) and O.L. (16th), and a total length of 6,020 yards (5505m). Only the railway separates it from another famous 18-hole course, the 6,458 yards (5905m) long championship course of the Maesdu Club, founded in 1915. The road bridge over the railway was built in 1931 to replace a level crossing, traces of which can still be seen. Prior to 1928 the road to Deganwy led from Alexandra Road, over the crossing and up over the shoulder of Bryn Gosol. The present main road follows the line of an old footpath through Maesdu farm.

Llandudno General Hospital, a 138-bed unit, stands on a slightly elevated site beside Maesdu golf course. It was opened by Princess Alice, daughter of Alice Liddell's paramour Prince Leopold, in August 1939, when it replaced the 40-bed Sarah Nicol Memorial Hospital (later the Youth Centre) in Trinity Avenue. Llandudno was a pioneer in the provision of hospital facilities. As early as 1875 Mrs. Goode, widow of the Dean of Ripon, was running the Cambrian Sanatorium, with the aid of voluntary donations, at Plas Llewelyn, in Llewelyn Avenue. This led to the opening, on 27 June 1881, of the first town hospital, with seven beds, in a rented house in Caroline Street. A year later Dr. and Mrs. James Nicol pioneered the scheme which led to the opening of the Sarah Nicol Memorial Hospital in May 1885 – Mrs. Nicol having died in February 1884, aged 66. Simultaneously with these developments the local authority pioneered the compulsory notification of infectious diseases in 1879, and in 1884 built a 50-bed isolation hospital in Maesdu Road, close to the level crossing. With the virtual elimination of such diseases as diphtheria the isolation hospital was closed in 1950 and subsequently converted into a 45-bed medical annexe for the use of the present general hospital. In the 1980s it became an EMI (elderly mentally infirm) centre. During a smallpox scare, round about 1910, a corrugated iron hospital was built on the site of the Maesdu clubhouse. This was taken over by the golf club as their first meeting place in 1928. Llandudno General Hospital became an outstandingly successful nurse training school in 1953, with full pass rates in the annual SRN examinations, but the school was closed in 1971 when matrons were abolished. The hospital was visited by Princess Marina, Duchess of Kent in 1960, and by her daughter, Princess Alexandra, in 1970 when she presented the annual prizes to the hospital's nurses. Her daughter, Marina Ogilvy, was admitted to the hospital as a patient on 6 February 1987 after a car crash near Glanconwy.

Bethel Independent Evangelical Church, in Mowbray Road, was built in 1901 by the Welsh Wesleyan Methodists who called it the Warren Mission. It was sold in 1913 to the English Wesleyans who, in turn, sold it to the Salvation Army.

1: Edith, Lorina and Alice Liddell, painted by Sir William Richmond at Llandudno in 1864. 2: Statue of Dean Liddell at Christ Church, Oxford. 3: Melissa Robinette in Alice costume beside the Lewis Carroll memorial font in Llandudno's West Shore church. 4: Alice and Edith Liddell photographed at the Llandudno studio of Thomas Edge.

Alice's philatelic wonderland.

Like all the early street names of the town, Lloyd Street is derived from the Mostyn family – Sir Edward Lloyd, of Pengwern, Flintshire. He inherited most of the estates of his bachelor brother-in-law, Sir Thomas Mostyn, in 1831, adopted the family name and was created the first Baron Mostyn in the same year.

Lloyd Street was intended to run from shore to shore, when first opened up in 1866, although its northern end is known as St. George's Place, taking its name from the hotel. No. 1 St. George's Place, currently Harmony House, was once the Prince of Wales Hotel, a name inherited from a pre-1848 squatter's homestead on the same site. The squatters earned their living from the sea and their boat, which was one of the first to provide trips for tourists, was called the *Prince of Wales*.

Crossing Mostyn Street into Lloyd Street proper, the HSBC Bank and adjacent properties mark the site of Bright Terrace, a row of houses named after the great Victorian politician John Bright (now 1, 2 and 3 Lloyd Street). The Rochdale reformer's long association with Llandudno began in 1864 when, after a somewhat stormy political season, he took his family on holiday to the St. George's Hotel. One afternoon, while strolling through St. Tudno's churchyard, five-years-old Leonard Bright exclaimed: "Oh, Mamma, when I am dead I want to be buried here." John Bright, then aged 53, and his wife Margaret, laughed at the child's innocent remark and they all returned to their hotel for tea. That night Leonard became ill, and within a week he died of scarlet fever. It was a heartbroken John Bright who walked to the Rectory in Church Walks, to ask if his son's last wish could be granted. "I readily assented and I have never forgotten Mr. Bright's expression of thanks, which I never looked for," recorded the Reverend John Morgan. A place for the grave was found near the church door, where a memorial wreath was laid a century later by eleven-years-old Delyth Rees, the youngest of the 775 pupils at John Bright Grammar School. John Bright visited his son's grave at least once a year until his own death in 1889. He became a familiar figure in Llandudno, addressed public meetings and provided pensions out of his income for some of the aged poor of the town.

Llandudno Town Hall stands on the opposite side of Lloyd Street, the product of a £50 prize in an architectural competition of 1894. Intended to be a £10,000 edifice in the English Renaissance style, it emerged eight years, two law suits and three builders later as a conglomeration of the stark and the flamboyant such as only the later Victorian architects were capable of producing. It was based on E.W. Mountford's design for Battersea Town Hall built in 1892, in a contrasting blend of white stone and red brick, in a Baroque form of Classicism. One of the first meetings to be held within its portals was a Government inquiry into the cost, which had risen to twice the original estimate. The foundation stone was laid on 26 October 1899 and the building was opened on 10 February 1902 by Alderman Sir Albert Rollitt, of Hull, and MP for South Islington. From the first meeting in the Council Chamber it was discovered that the acoustics were unsatisfactory – a problem which is still with us. Llandudno's memorial to Queen Victoria is in the form of a brass plaque in the foyer.

The former Ebeneser Welsh Methodist chapel, next door to the Town Hall, occupies the site of an English Wesleyan chapel built in 1861 and which moved to Mostyn Street, to become St. John's church in 1866. Welsh Methodism was founded at Llandudno at least as early as 1805, when the mining village was made part of the Beaumaris circuit. Caersalem chapel was opened in Cwlach Street in 1837, and was sold in 1873 to Richard Evans, of Haydock, so as to raise the money for the erection of Ebeneser, which was opened in June 1874. The present building was erected on the same site in 1909. (The congregation bought back Caersalem in 1889, reopened it as a mission of Ebeneser in 1892, closed it in 1934 and sold it in 1946). The chapel lease ended in March 1972, and unable to raise the money to buy the freehold, the congregation quit the site in 1975, moving into Rehoboth chapel in Trinity Avenue in 1982.

Breton Court, at 24 Lloyd Street, was the scene of Llandudno's first recorded murder, on 2 June 1970. John Thomas Davies, a 46-years-old factory worker, lodging in Clifton Road, twice stabbed 72-years-old Mrs. Florence Roberts, on his way through the house to attack a 43-years-old woman living upstairs. Mrs. Roberts died in a pool of blood on the front steps of her home, then known as Jubilee House, but the younger woman

recovered after hospital treatment. When taken off a bus, which had been intercepted by the police at Deganwy, Davies said: "I killed the wrong woman." He pleaded guilty to murder at Chester Assizes and was sentenced to life imprisonment.

Across the road stands the Roman Catholic Church of Our Lady Star of the Sea (Stella Maris), consecrated in November 1973, but opened sixty years earlier by the Bishop of Shrewsbury, in the presence of Cardinal Vaughan, Archbishop of Westminster, and Sir John Knill, Lord Mayor of London. Of the

A goat kid from the Great Orme herd seen with its bronze big brother off Berlin's Unter den Linden, after joining the 1st Battalion Royal Welch Fusiliers as regimental mascot in 1990. HMS Majestic, seen here at Birkenhead, was the resident coastguard ship in the Irish Sea to which the Llandudno gunners of the Royal Naval Artillery Volunteers were attached.

priests present at the opening, seven became bishops, including Francis Mostyn who became Bishop of Menevia in 1898 and Archbishop of Cardiff in 1921. It was at this church that John Petit was enthroned as Bishop of Menevia in 1947. The church was consecrated by Bishop Petit's successor, Bishop Langton Fox.

Lloyd Street School was opened in 1882 as the town's first board school. It has two foundation stones recording that they were laid in December 1881 by John Bright and William Rathbone. The latter was returned as Liberal MP for Caernarvonshire in 1880, and as MP for North Caernarvonshire when the county was divided into two constituencies (plus the Caernarvon Boroughs seat, which incorporated Llandudno) in 1885. He retained the seat until 1895 and died in 1902, aged 83. The school closed in October 1989, when the children were transferred to what is now called Tudno School, being the refurbished original higher grade/secondary modern school in Trinity Avenue. The old Lloyd Street building now houses the Conwy County Borough's archives.

The location of the lifeboat house, 700 yards (640m) away from its slipway on the northern promenade, always amazes strangers. When the building was erected beside the school, in 1903, Llandudno was much less developed than it is today and the intention was to place it midway between the two shores. The original lifeboat house of 1861 was erected beside the railway station to facilitate transporting the boat by train to Penmaenmawr and Colwyn Bay, which were to be served by the new Ormeshead crew, although the theory was never put into operation.

During the first half of the 19th century a thousand people were drowned in shipping mishaps within sight of Llandudno. In 1860 the Lifeboat Inspector visited the town, and his subsequent recommendation for the establishment of a new station coincided with a gift of £200 from two Liverpool sisters in memory of a third. They stipulated that the money was to be used to provide a lifeboat for Llandudno where all three had spent many happy holidays. They also asked for the boat to be called the *Sisters Memorial,* this being the first instance of a lifeboat being named by its donors. Their boat arrived by train on 8 January 1861 and was formally launched and named the next day by Lady Augusta Mostyn. (For more information about the Llandudno lifeboats, and the Llandudno maritime scene, see *Shipwrecks of North Wales,* by Ivor Wynne Jones, 2001).

Llandudno's first native centenarian, John Evans, told the author, on his hundredth birthday in November 1961, that as a young apprentice joiner he had helped to build the headquarters of the Llandudno unit of the Royal Naval Artillery Volunteer Reserve on the site of the lifeboat house. Describing it to the author, he said it was a replica of part of the gun deck of H.M.S. *Majestic,* complete with gun-ports and practice cannon. The *Majestic* served in the Crimean War and in 1860 was posted to Liverpool to serve as the resident coastguard warship for the Irish Sea.

Lloyd Street is now severed by The Oval, where cricket was introduced to the town in 1890. Prince Philip, Earl of Merioneth and Consort to Queen Elizabeth II, used it as a helicopter landing site when visiting the town in 1965. He had arrived by train on his first visit in 1963, when he accompanied the Queen to the National Eisteddfod, and he came by car to address a conference at the Winter Gardens in 1973. He returned again on 16 June 1993 to speak to the 2,500 people made homeless by a flash flood on the 10th. The isolated section of road beyond the Oval is now known as Lloyd Street West. Llandudno Urban Council acquired The Oval in 1949 and it is now the property of Conwy County Borough Council.

The framework for the 1896 Eisteddfod pavilion on the site of the present Post Office and Oriel Mostyn, in Vaughan Street. Llandudno's last gun, a 25-pounder, guarded by local Army cadets in the traditional uniforms of the Royal Garrison Artillery and Denbighshire Hussars, before leaving the town in September 1966.

Vaughan Street came into being in 1844 as Bay Street, being the path by which stones were taken from the beach to make Conwy Road. In June 1873 a company proposed to extend Vaughan Street seaward by means of a pier (without a landing stage), and the idea was revived briefly in 1895. The yacht jetty on the site was built in 1965.

Tudno Castle Hotel is a name restored in the 1990s for what was known for many decades as the North Western, which confused many people who thought the name was meant to describe its location. It was originally two separate units, the Tudno Castle Hotel to the north, and the Temperance Hotel nearest the station. Its most notorious guest was Igor Laptev, First Secretary at the Russian Embassy in London, who booked in with forty-two of his embassy staff in 1969, and with thirty a year later. In October 1971 the Foreign Office identified Laptev as a top Soviet spy and expelled him from Britain, along with 104 of his KGB colleagues. Russians seem to have an affinity for Vaughan Street; Alexander Soldatov, Soviet Deputy Foreign Minister during the 1971 incident, had stayed at the Imperial Hotel with his wife Rufina, and daughters Olga and Natalia, in 1965 when he was Ambassador in London.

A pavilion was erected in the street outside the North Western Hotel in June 1880, when the Prince of Wales (later King Edward VII) spent ten minutes in the town, arriving by train to turn on the new water supply from natural lakes Dulyn and Melinllyn, above the Conwy Valley. The Prince was on his way from Holyhead to the Staffordshire home of the Duke of Sutherland, who accompanied him to Llandudno. Previously the town had been supplied by natural springs and wells on the Great Orme which by 1864 were described as inadequate, by Robert Price, engineer and manager of the Llandudno Water & Gas Company. In 1875 the town Commissioners promoted a Bill which received Royal assent in August 1876 enabling them to acquire Dulyn, with a surface area of 36 acres (14.5 hectares), 1,747 feet (532m) above sea level, and Melinllyn, with 18 acres (7 hectares) at an altitude of 2,094 feet (638m), in a zone with an average annual rainfall of 96 inches (244cm). The pipes from the lakes crossed the River Conwy in a trench. The engineer for the scheme was Thomas T.Marks, founder of a prominent Llandudno family. A duplicate set of pipes was turned on in April 1909 by Lord Stalbridge, chairman of the London & North Western Railway Company, and who, as Richard Grosvenor, MP for Flintshire, had been at the 1880 ceremony. In 1965 the Llandudno water undertaking, the envy of many a town, was merged with neighbouring schemes in the Conwy Valley Water Board, which eventually became part of the Welsh Water Authority, and was subsequently privatised. Until 1965 Llandudno water was so cheap that new residents were required to deposit £1 with the council – to cover their quarterly bill if they should leave the town without paying.

On the opposite corner of the intervening Conwy Road the six-storey block of shops and flats, opened in 1996 as Marlborough Place, stands on the site of the pioneering Red Garage and Motor Showroom from 1904 until 1988, stretching back into Argyll Road. The garage and adjoining head Post Office were built on the land used for the 10,000-seat pavilion of the 1896 National Eisteddfod, in which Sir Arthur Stepney, of Llanelli, presented the Gorsedd of Bards with the banner they still carry. Another notable event of this Eisteddfod was Sir Hubert von Herkomer's revelation of his designs for the present crown, breastplate, sword and robes of the Archdruid. Describing the significance of the regalia, Sir Hubert said: "The breast plate will choke the Archdruid if he enters a wrong judgment." The Red Garage was demolished in 1989.

The Post Office remains, although the sorting office at the rear was moved to bigger premises in Maesdu Road in October 1998. It was opened on 20 May 1904 by Lord Stanley, the Postmaster General, who said it was the biggest and best equipped in North Wales. "The postal business in Llandudno is the third largest in the whole of Wales, being exceeded only by Cardiff and Newport," he said, adding that an average of 173,000 letters a week were posted via the former Gloddaeth Street Post Office (and Sorting Office) in 1903. By 2002 Llandudno Post Office was handling 60,000 letters a day – 1,300,000 were handled in the two-week Christmas period of 2001. Before the days of ubiquitous telephones Post Office telegrams were an important means of fast communication and 120,000 were handled in Llandudno during 1903.

Oriel Mostyn, next door to the Post Office, was founded in 1902 to display the private collection of Lady Augusta Mostyn, widow of Thomas Edward Lloyd Mostyn (1830-61), and daughter of the Earl of Abergavenny. In 1914 the gallery was requisitioned for use as an Army drill hall, after which it became a warehouse. It was again requisitioned in World War Two for use as an Inland Revenue storeroom, and reverted to commercial use as a piano store. Artist Sir Kyffin Williams discovered the building in 1976, to begin a campaign for its restoration to its original use. It reopened as a public gallery in 1979, as a display area for a series of temporary exhibitions.

In order to extend Vaughan Street to the first railway station, in 1858, a "long barrow," or Stone Age burial mound had to be removed. (A similar mound was demolished in the vicinity of the lighthouse during the construction of Marine Drive). The present frontage to the station was built in 1891-92. Its five platforms embraced features of a major terminal, such as the long road between platforms 2 and 3, enabling Hansom cabs to line up alongside the railway carriages. Just outside the station there were enormous balloon sidings – eleven sidings to the west and nine to the east, where trains, arriving every four minutes at peak excursion periods, were taken for cleaning, coaling and watering for their return journeys. There was a turntable near Maesdu Bridge, on which locomotives were turned around to head in the right direction for their return journeys.

It was in these sidings, behind Kings Road, that the Royal train was parked soon after midnight on 8 August 1963, ready to steam into Llandudno the following morning for the first visit to the town by a reigning British monarch, Queen Elizabeth II. These sidings were removed during the two years following the substitution of diesel locomotives in 1966. One of the last steam engines to visit Llandudno was the famous *Flying Scotsman*, on 4 June 1966. Platforms 4 and 5 were closed in 1978. The entire station was covered with a glass canopy, which was removed in 1990.

From 1907 to 1942 the Clubman train left Llandudno at 7.40am every weekday, for local businessmen working in Manchester. Members of the Club had permanent seats, on which their regular newspapers would be waiting, and each had a locker on the train. They were served a wide variety of breakfasts at their seats, and there was a waiting list for membership. While the special Clubman carriages were removed during the war, the 7.40am Llandudno-Manchester train continued until 1965, and was still called the Clubman.

A Patriot class locomotive, built at Derby in 1932 as No. 5954, was officially named *Llandudno* at the station on 12 May 1938. Thirty-two years later her nameplate was presented to the town – the engine having been scrapped in 1962. While in service it covered 1,359,576 miles, mainly on the Liverpool-London, Manchester-London and Liverpool-Leeds lines. The engine weighed 80 tons 15 cwts, and its tender a further 42 tons 14 cwts.

Vaughan Street terminates in a T-junction at the railway station, the branch to the right is Augusta Street, leading straight into Madoc Street, while the branch to the left is Oxford Road. This is where Llandudno Police Station and Magistrates' Court was built in 1915 and extended in 1961, when it became the Conwy Division HQ of the three-county Gwynedd Police. In 1968 its jurisdiction was extended to the River Dyfi, in Cardigan Bay, as one of the four divisional offices of the new North Wales Police. The Court moved to a new building in Conwy Road in 1993, and the

Police Station is currently the Central Coastal Divisional Headquarters, for the area from Llanfairfechan to Prestatyn, and south to Betws-y-coed, although there are proposals to replace it with a new divisional HQ at St. Asaph. It is also the area custody station.

The brick building opposite the Police Station was built as stables for the 150 horses and varied fleet of the Llandudno Coaching & Carriage Company. The last of the horses was sold in 1918 to make way for Royal Blue buses, who sold out to Crosville in 1931. When Crosville moved out in 1971 the vibrations of closing the door for the last time brought down a shower of chaff from hidden cavities, fifty-three years after the last delivery of hay!

The road opposite Oxford House (the former 1926 maternity home previously mentioned) is now called Norman Road but until recently was Council Street, a reminder that the town's first nineteen "workmen's dwellings" were built here in 1897, at a cost of £210 each. They are still lived in although now refurbished to make attractive modern homes. Another early Council housing scheme is commemorated on a plaque low down on the wall of 35 Kings Road, inscribed: "Llandudno Housing Scheme 1920. This stone was laid by Mrs. D. Lloyd George, the wife of the Prime Minister, 8 October 1920."

Oxford Road leads to John Bright School, opened on 25 September 1907 by Whitelaw Reid, United States Ambassador in London. Rate-aided secondary education came to Llandudno in 1893 with a system of bursaries to pay rail fares for a limited number of boys to attend Friars School, Bangor, while girls were sent to Caernarfon County School – the first Intermediate (Grammar) School in Wales. A local school (now the Risboro Hotel) was opened in 1896 in Clement Avenue, with annual fees of £7 to £8 for tuition, 6s (30p) for stationery, 5s (25p) for athletics, £4/10/0d (£4.50) for music and £35 extra for boarders. The sexes were segregated until July 1901 when two girls joined the boys to sit the annual matriculation examination for university. One of the girls was Gladys Morgan, sister of the man who became Archbishop Morgan. By 1905 there were 82 pupils and steps were taken to build new premises in Oxford Road, aided by a local fund which had been launched in 1889 with the original intention of commemorating John Bright with a statue. The

headmaster from 1896 until his death, aged 57, in 1912 was J.M. Archer Thomson, a famous mountaineer. On the school balcony, around the entrance hall, there is a plaque recording: "The equipment of these laboratories was given by the Court of the Drapers' Company as a mark of their consideration for the Headmaster, a Liveryman of the Company. AD 1910."

Llandudno was flooded in June 1993 when 5¹/₂ inches of rain fell in three hours that coincided with high tide. The water backed up beyond the Links Hotel, behind the trees to the right of this photograph taken in Conwy Road.

He was succeeded by C. Madoc Jones 1913-43, and S.O. Rees in 1943, after which John Bright became a comprehensive school under F. Garfield Rees who had been headmaster of the secondary modern (originally "higher grade") school in Trinity Avenue. Mr. Rees retired in 1975 and was replaced by Gareth Jones who, after his retirement, became one of the founder members of the National Assembly for Wales inaugurated in May 1999 (after elections the previous year, when he stood for the Welsh Nationalist Party, Plaid Cymru). His successor was Mrs. Irene Scott-Perry, who took over in 1994. An arsonist seriously damaged the school's assembly hall on 11 December 1985. At the time of writing there are controversial plans to replace the present building with a new school on the old gasworks site, in Maesdu Road, with adjoining playing fields on the old seagull-infested refuse tip on the former Creuddyn swamp, closed about a quarter of a century ago and now grassed over.

In August 1969 a committee of teachers at John Bright School took the controversial pioneering step of banishing the wearing of gymslips and dark stockings, in favour of white blouses, 16 inch (41cm) mini skirts, skin-coloured tights or white knee-length stockings, for all girls aged from 11 to 18. This was at a time when the local shops reported the average mini skirt sold in Llandudno to be 18 inches (46cm) .

Behind John Bright School, in Cwm Road, stands Ysgol Morfa Rhianedd, opened on 12 July 1963, as the town's first permanent Welsh junior school. After two years of agitation and public meetings the school was founded, with sixteen pupils, on 2 May 1949, in an abandoned Army Nissen hut beside Conwy Road. There were 80 pupils on the books when the present building was opened by Sir Ben Bowen Thomas, Permanent Secretary at the Welsh Department of the Ministry of Education, who unveiled a commemorative plaque. The school lost its roof in a gale during the early hours of 17 January 1993, when its timbers were hurled 100 yards (91m), seriously damaging houses across the road.

Augusta Street is short and contains nothing of interest. It links up with Trinity Square (containing an 1894 horse trough, given by Mrs. William Jenkins, of Birmingham) and Trinity Avenue, with the old Youth Centre on the right (see Chapter 3, More stylish than some) and Albion Street on the left, leading into Jubilee Street. The latter houses were completed in 1887 by the Llandudno Workingmen's Dwelling Company, which was formed a year earlier as Britain's first tontine of its kind (and is still in being). In 1920 the same tontine built Dinas Road and part of Winllan Avenue. Three houses in Jubilee Street (originally called Warehouse Street) retain the shape of the first Rehoboth Welsh Presbyterian mission, built in 1883 and replaced in March 1894 by the chapel in Trinity Avenue (which bears the date of 1893). After 1967 Rehoboth also served as the home of the English Baptists, who lost their own place of worship in Mostyn Street when the lease expired, and since 1982 has accommodated the Welsh Wesleyan Methodists who renamed it Ebeneser, after their original church in Lloyd Street.

A house called Hafod Wen, in Caroline Road (opposite Rehoboth) is notable as the place where Mrs. Elizabeth Davies died in August 1970. She was the mother of Miss Winnie Davies, the Llandudno missionary who was shot in the Congolese jungle in May 1967, after three years of torture and humiliation as the slave of an African rebel who called himself General Ngalo.

While proceeding from Augusta Street past the horse trough, a glance at the NFU Insurance offices in Trinity Square reminds one that they occupy the site of the Llandudno Convalescent Home for Women, opened in 1869. It had been closed for some years when pressed into service in 1956 as a hostel for refugees who escaped from Hungary when the Soviet army crushed the brief anti-communist uprising.

Madoc Street came into being as an ingenious gesture by which Mostyn Estates removed most of the squatters from the choice land which now makes up the Promenade and Mostyn Street. As noted in Chapter 2 (St. George's Harbour), there were about twenty-five homesteads on the Common at the passing into law of the 1843 Enclosure Act. If they had stayed put on the Common the squatters would have been recognised by the 1893 Land Commission as having a claim to their holdings, under the ancient Welsh custom of the *tŷ unos* (meaning "one-night house"). A similar practice had existed in England where a squatter on common land acquired a freehold if he had not been challenged for twelve years. In Wales a squatter who could build a house complete with roof, and have smoke rising through the chimney and a meal on the table, all between sunset and sunrise, acquired a title. At dawn he stood against each of the four corners, and threw an axe, the four landing points marking his boundary. The ditches by which the squatters drained their holdings usually exaggerated their boundaries while also improving their land. The Llandudno homesteads had been in existence for many years without hindrance but, as a preliminary to the 1848 apportionment of the Common, the Mostyn agent managed to extract a nominal rent from all but five of the squatters. This enforced recognition of a pseudo-title for which a tenancy rent was paid, paved the way for the removal of the squatters, and as further inducement to go quietly nominal leases of five shillings (25p) a year were offered to those who agreed to move into a row of new cottages specially built in Madoc Street.

The squatters were still on the Common at the time of the 1851 census but ten years later they were all well established in Madoc Street where nine were listed as boatmen and six as miners. They included Richard Hughes, at No. 13. Born in Anglesey in 1816, he worked in the Amlwch copper mines before moving to Llandudno, where he built a substantial homestead beside what is now Mostyn Street. When Llandudno began to develop he became a road contractor and later formed the syndicate that built Marine Drive. He was the treasurer of Tabernacl Welsh Baptist chapel for many years, keeping their money in a tin embedded in the hot ashes beneath his kitchen grate – there being no bank at Llandudno in those days. Richard Hughes was also the first bathing machine owner in the town.

The tunnel, sometimes known as Marble Arch, leading from Madoc Street into St. Mary's Road preserves what was once the entrance to the private farmland belonging to St. George's Hotel.

An October 1902 progress inspection during the building of what is now the North Wales Medical Centre, in Queen's Road.

A distant view of early Craig-y-don, from Bodafon.
In the picture below one of the town's first trams is descending Penrhyn Hill.

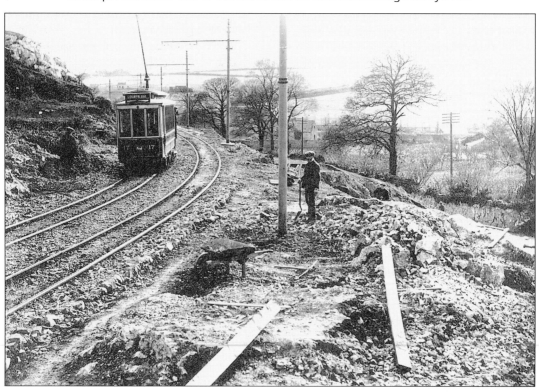

CRAIG-Y-DON

18

After walking a few yards past the North Wales Theatre on the promenade, or the Grand Theatre in Mostyn Broadway, one arrives at Craig-y-don – a name derived from Craig-y-don near Beaumaris, the home of Thomas Peers Williams (1795-1875). As owner of Marl he was allocated 30 acres (12 hectares) of the Llanrhos Common and 28 acres (11 hectares) in Llandudno, under the 1848 Enclosure Award. One crosses the diocesan boundary between Bangor and St. Asaph while walking to Craig-y-don. There were vague proposals for matching the two North Wales bishoprics to the enlarged county boundaries created in the 1974 reorganisation of local government, but the idea had to be scrapped after yet another set of local government changes in 1996 which straddled the medieval boundary between Caernarvonshire and Denbighshire.

Early development of Craig-y-don was confined to the top of Nant-y-gamar Road where, in Coed Gaer, the woods overlooking Gloddaeth, there are the readily distinguishable remains of ancient stone hut circles and burial chambers – as implied by the Welsh name Coed Gaer. There is a 1618 record of Sir Thomas Mostyn's building a windmill on land belonging to Gloddaeth, and a windmill in this vicinity was delineated in Lewis Morris chart of Conwy Estuary, in 1748, as a landmark to aid navigation. However, the folk memory preserves the name Hen Dŵr for the present structure, and that translates as Old Tower. One of the oldest roads in Penrhynside, on the other side of the mountain, is called Hen Dŵr Lane. The isolated structure had clearly long ceased to be a windmill and was probably derelict by the time it was taken over by the Crown for use as an invasion warning beacon during the Napoleonic Wars, after which it was described simply as the Old Tower (not Old Mill).

It was the Bodafon Mountain Beacon mentioned in a letter about the intended construction of a matching beacon on one of the hilltops of what we now call Colwyn Bay, written by Thomas Ellis, of Rhosfynach, on 7 April 1804: "My coadjutator and I contracted for the building of the Hut for the sum allowed by Government, viz £10. We have not finished the Beacon. It will cost us about the same sum as the hut – taking into account the firing materials. We, like you, Sir, are not at all satisfied with the execution of the Hut. It has been made a job of, as most Government matters are. However the Hut will stand our Llandudno storms and that was our greatest aim," wrote Ellis.

"If agreeable to you," he wrote to John Lloyd, of Wigfair, St. Asaph, "and you judge it worthy trial, I would propose that we write to the Superintendents of the Bodafon Mountain Beacon and solicit them to fire a small quantity of materials on a given night and hour, which, if seen by us, shall be repeated by us to you. It is essential that we make ourselves competent to the trust committed to us in so momentous a period and state of our country."

There was some 19th century quarrying at the top of Nant-y-gamar road, during which valuable beds of white china clay were discovered and exploited. The clay was taken down to the beach and loaded into flat-bottomed boats that were lifted by the incoming tide for shipping to Runcorn.

The first building on the Craig-y-don seafront was Ascot, a large house built in the 1870s at the eastern corner of what became Carmen Sylva Road, and demolished in March 1974. It stood in isolation until June 1884 when the Craig-y-don Estate sold the freehold of 2,210 acres (895 hectares) over a period of three days, involving Llandudno, Llandudno Junction, Conwy and Colwyn Bay. Mostyn Estate retained the intervening area now known as Bodafon Fields, and in 1888 auctioned thirteen plots on which most of the houses in Bodafon Lane were built, on land described as Bodafon, Yr Aber and Erw Coed. Bodafon farm was the home of the Mostyn land agent.

Eryl Fryn was the home of Sir William Letts, a director of Crossley Motors, who bought it in 1922. He was one of the founders of the Automobile Association. During the earliest years of the motorcar he and his business partner Charles Jarrott-Wright used their employees to warn drivers of police speed traps. These pioneers formed the first bicycle patrols of the AA when it was founded in June 1905. People visiting Lady Letts were usually invited to join her in a game of croquet on the lawn at the rear. Sir William died in 1959.

The attraction of the Craig-y-don freeholds, as opposed to the Mostyn leaseholds, resulted in rapid development and within a year Riddell & Jarvis' public tennis ground was opened where St. David's English Methodist church now stands. Lawn tennis was still relatively new, having been invented by Major Walter Wingfield, at Nantclwyd Hall, Llanelidan, near Ruthin, in 1873. Llandudno established a tennis tradition and in 1912 J. C. Parke, a local solicitor, played in the singles, and J. C. Parke and A. E. Beamish in the doubles, when Britain won the Davis Cup. This pioneering court is now no more than a memory preserved in the name "Tennis Court" on a house at 32 Victoria Street, overlooking the site. The Queen's Road tennis courts were opened in 1931.

Craig-y-don's biggest building is St. Paul's church – and since 1970 its members have been perturbed by repeated suggestions that it is a memorial to Jack the Ripper, the mysterious figure who cruelly murdered six London prostitutes in 1888. Modern criminologists have assembled circumstantial evidence to show the Ripper could have been Prince Albert Victor, Duke of Clarence, and heir to the Prince of Wales. The Duke died in 1892, aged 28, the victim of oysters that had been travelling around the country for several days, without refrigeration, after being harvested at Beaumaris. In 1891 the Bishop of St. Asaph had highlighted the need for a church to serve English visitors to this fast-growing area, and in 1893 work began on the construction of the Duke of Clarence Memorial Church at Craig-y-don. An inscribed memorial stone was laid on 10 April 1895 by the Duchess of Teck, who was accompanied by the Duke and their daughter, the Princess Mary, who having been engaged to the Duke of Clarence, married his brother in 1893 and later became Queen Mary (wife of George V). The south aisle, added in 1899, was the gift of John Walker, of Osborne House, North Parade. He also gave the spectacular eagle lectern. His daughter Jeannette was the wife of the Reverend Francis Griffith Jones, Vicar of Llanrhos, who was responsible for overseeing the construction (and lived at 8 Mostyn Street). The church was completed with the addition of the present chancel in August 1901, the gift of Lady Augusta Mostyn, and was consecrated by Bishop Alfred George Edwards (who became the first Archbishop of the Church in Wales). The east window is a memorial to Lady Augusta.

When Mostyn Broadway was being extended from the Grand Theatre to St. Paul's church, in January 1907, someone spotted several Roman coins among the rubble washed by overnight rain. A search produced over a hundred coins outside the church, and another 452 at the source of the rubble, opposite the stable entrance to what is now the Craigside Inn (or Brewsters), at Craigside. Most of those recovered bore the effigy of Carausius, and were minted in London and Colchester in the period 287-293. A.D. Half-a-mile to the east of the source, beside the same roadway over the Little Orme, another 5,000 Roman coins were found in an earthenware jar in 1873. Two thirds of them belonged to the reign of Constantine the Great, 306–337 A.D, and others ranged backwards in time to 286 A.D, with numerous European mint marks. It is conjectured that the hoards must have been associated with the Llandudno copper mines.

From St. Paul's church to Nant-y-gamar the main road is known as Mostyn Avenue. In the days of the Llandudno & Colwyn Bay Electric Railway, 1907-56, the trams used to travel up the main street and across Nant-y-gamar into the fields leading to Penrhynside. The abandoned track was given a temporary surface and used as a road to the 1963 National Eisteddfod, on Bodafon Fields.

Sandy Macpherson at the console of the BBC theatre organ while it was evacuated to Llandudno's Grand Theatre in 1940. It is now at Pasadena, California. Below is Robert Loraine's aircraft on Penrhyn Bay & Rhos-on-Sea golf course in August 1910 – the first aircraft to land in Wales.

It attracted an attendance of 138,000, including the Queen and Prince Philip. This was one of the rare eisteddfodau where the judges could not find a bard worthy of the chair, but the crown was awarded to Tom Parri-Jones. Oddly the reverse had been the case when the eisteddfod previously visited Llandudno in 1896. During the course of the 1963 festival the author received a personal greeting from President Gamal abd-el Nasser, of Egypt, to be read to the military veterans of the 1943 Cairo Eisteddfod, who were meeting for a twentieth anniversary reunion.

The North Wales school for physically handicapped children (Ysgol Gogarth), beside the old tram track, was opened on 10 September 1962 by athlete Chris Chataway.

Carmen Sylva Road, Roumania Drive, Sylva Gardens and similar street names in Craig-y-don commemorate the 1890 visit of Queen Elisabeth of Romania, but Queen's Road is named after Queen Victoria. It is the main intersection at Craig-y-don. Benards' shop at No. 43 was the site of Revill Hall's 1,000-seat marquee, erected in 1914 when his pierrots had to leave the Princes Theatre. By the end of the year it had been taken over as an emergency military hospital. English Methodists later built a corrugated-iron chapel on the site before moving to their present St. David's church. The Evangelical church in Queen's Road was opened as a Welsh Baptist chapel in 1894. Lady Augusta Mostyn bought it in 1910 and gave the Baptists land to enable them to expand their 1889 Salem mission (now belonging to the Christadelphians) in 1912 at the opposite end of Mostyn Broadway. Lady Augusta then presented the Queen's Road building to the parish church and it was known as St. Paul's Church House until again sold in 1974, when a new Church House was built in the garden of St. Paul's.

The carpet warehouse next door to the Evangelical church used to have an inscription over the entrance: "Livery Stables, 1902." It was hacked off in 1957 to make way for two short-lived lamps advertising BP petrol, on what was then a garage and petrol station – founded by a son of Dr. Thomas, of the Hydro Hotel. A small stone garage on the opposite side of the road was built in 1899 and inscribed "Fire Station." It was once equipped with a small horse-drawn manually operated pump, to serve the Craig-y-don area.

A network of roads tucked away behind the old Livery Stables was where Craig-y-don School was established in 1902. The project was delayed because of the absence of sewers in the area, the Llandudno School Board's noting, in April 1900, that a number of new houses "have to depend upon the antiquated and unsatisfactory cesspool system." This, said the Board, was a blot on the fair name of Llandudno, and it called upon the Urban District Council to resolve the problem quickly.

By 1970 the school had become inadequate for the number of pupils, who overflowed into a couple of portable cabins in the yard, but when Caernarvonshire Education Committee, sitting in faraway Caernarfon, considered the matter in the October, they decided to defer any replacement "because the projected rate of housing development in the vicinity does not justify the inclusion of the project in the 1971-72 programme." Director of Education Mansel Williams said the authority would proceed with the acquisition of a new three-acre (1 hectare) site, "to the south of Clarence Drive (which links Conwy Road with Clarence Road), and to the west of Clarence Road," on land owned by Mostyn Estates. His lengthy explanation of the meaning of Clarence Drive was made necessary because most old residents then described the newly widened road as Jackson's Lane, a reference to Ben Jackson whose stables survived until the 1970s opposite the Links Hotel. The move to the new school was eventually made in 1977.

The estate behind the school is called Liddell Park, after Alice Liddell of *Wonderland* fame. In 1977 the developers invited the author to name the streets, and for the first five cul-de-sacs he chose Alice Gardens, Lorina's Lane, Isis Way, Cuffnells Close and Emery Down – the initial letters spelling ALICE. Llandudno Town Council made some meddlesome changes, substituting Lorina Grove for Lorina's Lane, and Isis Court for Isis Way. No one asked the significance of the names, which remain a mystery to some of the residents. Lorina was a sister of Alice, for whom Lewis Carroll composed his famous story during a boat ride on the River Isis; Cuffnells was the name of Alice's married home (now demolished) at Emery Down, in the New Forest. The author had matching ideas for the projected remaining roads, which would have emphasised the town's genuine links with the Liddell family, while steering clear of the myth of Lewis Carroll's supposed visit. Alas, the Town Council decided to name all future streets and created the trite and irrelevant Lewis Close, Dodgson Close, Daresbury Close, Queen's Way and Carpenter Avenue. Presumably the Council had failed to spot the acrostic in the first five names.

The house Dolarfon, in Roumania Drive, earned international notoriety in 1969 as the base from which former bank clerk Richard Williams took on the Establishment by printing his own Welsh money. This resulted in the Government's abolition, within a few months, of the blue 2d tax stamp which had to be embossed on every cheque and promissory note. Having printed his £1 and 10s notes he managed, after a delay of several hours, to have them taxed at the Liverpool Stamp Office, thus legalising them with the royal crown. A few days later the Government apologised for having illegally endorsed promissory notes for less than £5, and invited him to return his Welsh money for a refund of the tax – resulting in bank note collectors from all over the world wanting to buy his money, causing rapidly inflating second-hand prices. Mr. Williams responded by printing a single note for £1,000,000. When the Stamp Office objected he said it was for a sum in excess of the stipulated £5, which the London Establishment eventually conceded. He promptly stamped it "Cancelled" and auctioned it in London for several hundreds of pounds, as the first and last Government-endorsed Welsh million pound note. (The full story is told in the book *Money for All*, by Ivor Wynne Jones).

Queen's Road joins up with Fferm Bach Road, which was the earliest route from Llanrhos to Llandudno, via Nant-y-gamar. Rapallo House museum and art gallery was once situated in Fferm Bach Road. It was the private home and collection of Francis Chardon who bequeathed it to the town upon his death in 1925, aged 60. Rapallo was the maiden name of his mother, a daughter of Signor A.M. Rapallo who, by means of ships and personal wealth, was reputed to have helped elevate Louis Napoleon from President of the French Second Republic to Emperor of the Second Empire in 1852. The Rapallo House collection was moved in November 1985 to form the core of the present Llandudno Museum, in Gloddaeth Street.

Beyond the junction the North Wales Medical Centre (opened in June 1979) was built as Lady Forester's Convalescent Home, endowed in her will in memory of her husband General George Cecil Weld, 3rd Baron Forester, MP for Wenlock 1828-74, Comptroller of the Royal Household in 1852 and 1858-59. Born in 1807, Lord Forester was married in 1862 to the Hon. Mary Anne (who died in 1893), widow of Colonel D.O. Dyce Sombre, and only surviving daughter of Edward Jarvis, the 2nd Viscount St.Vincent. The first sod for the impressive building was cut on 17 January 1898, but construction did not begin until 1901, and it was 24 July 1902 before the foundation stone was laid, by Emma Georgina, wife of the 5th Baron. It was built to provide free accommodation to poor convalescents from Much Wenlock and Broseley. Aberconwy Borough Council (created in 1974) tried to buy the building in 1977 for conversion into their headquarters.

Continuing up the hill past the Medical Centre, into Tan-y-bryn Road, a plaque on one of the gateposts of Tan-y-bryn nursing home reminds us that this was once a school. It is inscribed: "These gates were erected in memory of old Tan-y-bryn boys who gave their lives for their country, 1914-1918."

Tollgates once guarded both entrances to Penrhyn Bay from Colwyn Bay. The one above was at the junction of Llandudno Road and Llanrhos Road until 1921. The one below was on the seafront, where the toll was collected until 1963.

19

Penrhyn Bay became part of the Llandudno Urban District upon the dissolution and redistribution of the old Conway Rural District in 1935, two years after Colwyn Bay abandoned its claims to an attractive area coveted as a natural extension to Rhos-on-Sea. Llandudno's rival claim relied upon the 1284 boundaries of Edward I, making the Afon Ganol (meaning "Middle River") the eastern extremity of the Principality of Wales (except for the detached Llysfaen area, which Edward perceived as having strategic value, and which became a part of Denbighshire in 1923).

This modern community is an overspill from the older Penrhynside, and both take their names from Penrhyn (now the licensed club and restaurant called Penrhyn Old Hall), the ancient house that is even older than the date of 1590 shown over one of the fireplaces, although the exact age is unknown. The part known as the Baronial Hall is at least as old as the reign of Henry VI. It was the home of generations of the Pugh family until sold to the Williamses of Craig-y-don (near Beaumaris) in 1760. The Pughs were staunch Catholics and it is sad to see their 16th century chapel decaying northeast of the house. According to the Royal Commission on Ancient & Historical Monuments in Wales, who hacked their way through the undergrowth to inspect it in 1951, this may be the building described in an inventory of 1535 as *Libera Capella Beatae Mariae de Penrhyn*, the free chapel of the Blessed Mary of Penrhyn. Three centuries later it was being used as a stable but in 1926 it was restored by the Church in Wales and used for regular Anglican worship until the erection of a corrugated-iron building in St. David's Road in 1930. The ancient Penrhyn chapel then became a youth club for a few years, and one can still see dart marks on one of the walls. The 1930 St. David's church was replaced in 1963 by the modern building beside Glan-y-mor Road, after which the corrugated iron building was demolished in 1985 and replaced with houses.

It was in a cave on the Little Orme, forming part of the Penrhyn property, that Robert Pugh assisted a group of priests to print *Y Drych Cristionogawl* ("The Christian Mirror") in 1585. Although the title page of this all-Welsh 180-page volume says it was published in Rouen, France, that was mere subterfuge to conceal the first printing of a book in Wales. Only three copies are known to have survived. Among the priests sheltered at Penrhyn was Father William Davies, of Groes-yn-Eirias (Colwyn Bay), who was hanged, drawn and quartered at Beaumaris Castle in July 1593, one of his severed hands being preserved at Penrhyn until the 19th century. He had been found guilty of being a Roman Catholic priest who had failed to quit the country within forty days of the passing of the Act of 27 Elizabeth Cap.2, and therefore guilty of treason. He was born in 1555 somewhere in the vicinity of Eirias Park, Colwyn Bay, from where he left for St. Edmund Hall, Oxford, in 1575. In 1582 he was admitted to Douai seminary – by then moved to Rheims, where he was ordained in 1585, just a week after Queen Elizabeth signed the Act under which he was eventually to be executed. Nine weeks later he left France to conduct his secret mission, in his own language, among his own people, hence his arrival at Penrhyn.

It was not until 14 April 1587, two years after the date in the imprint of *Y Drych Cristionogawl*, that the cave was discovered by a local man who chanced to come upon twelve priests, one or two of them armed with pistols. He immediately went to Gloddaeth to inform Sir Thomas Mostyn, who conscripted a *posse comitatus* of forty men to seek out the cave. This Wild West style *ad hoc* police force did not dare to enter the cave, "the mouth thereof was soe narrowe," wrote Dr. William Griffith, a Justice of the Peace for Caernarvonshire. Griffith's full account is contained in a letter he wrote to the Archbishop of Canterbury two days later. Mostyn's men stood guard all night but by daybreak the outlaws had vanished. The posse found the cave to be boarded and furnished with an altar, and it contained food and drink. Griffith said they discovered lead type scattered on the sea-washed beach below the cave, some of which was dispatched with his letter by way of evidence.

In 1962 Douglas B. Hague, an architect and archaeologist on the staff of the Royal Commission on Ancient and Historical Monuments In Wales, went in search of the cave, using a hazardous path from the west. On entering a hole some 2 ft high (0.6m), on a northern cliff overlooking the sea, he found a narrow fissure 7 ft (2m) long, which opened out to the right into a roughly round natural chamber with a diameter of 12 ft (3.6m), and matching height. In the wall was a niche that might have been cut to hold lanterns, and there were what appeared to be bearings cut into the rock for three joists, to support a boarded floor and give a level surface for a printing press. Excavation of the floor produced rough hollows that would have accommodated such joists. This, said Hague, would account for the contemporary description of the cave's having been "boarded" (rather than the modern misinterpretation stating the cave walls were lined with wood). Interestingly, Hague found a 15 ft (4.6m) long shaft rising southeast from the chamber, which would account for the escape of the priests while the mouth of the cave was being watched.

The author was a guest at the Vatican on 22 November 1987 when William Davies was beatified by Pope John Paul II, together with two other Welshmen (Richard Flower, hanged at Tyburn in 1588, and Humphrey Pritchard, hanged at Oxford in 1599). It was probably the first time for the Welsh language to be used in St Peter's Basilica, in spoken prayer and in the printed order of service. (The author's copy of the order of service was deposited at Llandudno Library for public reference). Davies had been investigated for beatification (the first step towards sainthood) since 1929, when he was designated Venerable. His name was resubmitted in 1978, and nine years later his title became the Blessed.

Man colonised the Little Orme at least 5,570 years ago, the proof being found in the carbon dating of a woman's skeleton found during quarrying in 1891. Removal of the rock face exposed what had been a very deep natural fissure, down which the woman had either fallen or been thrown. The hole had gradually filled with debris so that much higher up there were completely unrelated Bronze Age finds of around 1800 BC. These included a well-made bronze spearhead about a foot (0.3m) long and the bones of extinct British animals such as the rhinoceros and bear.

Earlier quarrying had taken place on the cliffs overlooking Penrhyn Hill but the main operation, on the other side of the headland, began in 1889 and continued until 1936. It was served until 1931 by a 3 ft (0.9m) gauge railway, operating on three levels, with the crushing mill and hoppers on the middle floor – designed for gravity loading into ships at a pier immediately below. There was a rope-worked incline to the top, and a locomotive-operated incline to the lower level. Eight locomotives operated in the quarry over the years, the oldest, named Mona, having begun its working life on the Isle of Man, before passing first to the Penmaenmawr granite quarry and then on to Penrhyn Bay. Many residents can remember the associated buildings, including those of the 1927 modernisation that survived until long after World War Two. One can still see traces of the hoppers but the pier has long gone.

A complex witchcraft altar was found on the site, at the top of White Chapel Bay, in January 1972. It had been recently used, perhaps the night before, because the fine ash of a wood fire had not had a chance to blow away, and a discarded pair of knickers had not been affected by weather. Satanic symbols and letters had been painted on the upright stone, which is still in place. The discovery resulted in a complaint to the *Daily Post* by a well-known Penrhyn Bay woman who said a policeman had called at her house, asking if she could interpret the inscriptions for his report!

There is a public footpath into the quarry (with a branch to the top of the Little Orme) from Penrhyn Hill – where three successive tiers of road are in use, the top section running through an old quarry that used to belong to the Craig-y-don Estate. The bottom level is the original track, the middle tier was laid to create a new road in 1921, and the top tier was cut in 1907 as a track bed for the Llandudno & Colwyn Bay Electric Railway. During the making of the tram track a man-made tunnel was discovered, penetrating deep into the Little Orme, and prompting the suggestion that it was a secret passage from the house to the cave of the 16th century printing press. The tunnel's entrance was soon covered and largely forgotten until December 1969, when it again came to light during the creation of the present dual carriageway (which opened in June 1972). As part of the work it was necessary to wall off the lane that ran from the middle road, across the tram track, to Pentre Isaf. It was while making this wall that the tunnel entrance was found, ten feet lower than the tram track and partially hidden by the surface of the 1921 road.

Resident road engineer Leo Scheltinga entered the tunnel, which he found was between four and five feet (1.2-1.5m) high, and three to five feet (0.9-1.5m) wide. He negotiated a rock fall halfway and found the tunnel ran almost in a straight line for 315 feet (96m). It terminated in a deep shaft. "The shaft is full of beautifully clear water, and part way down I could see the entrance to another tunnel heading in the direction of Llandudno, at about right angles to the main tunnel," he told the author. He believed the tunnel to be an abortive 19th century mineral exploration venture. He arranged for the first 50 feet (15m) to be filled, to obviate any risk of future subsidence.

The Little Orme, rising to over 400 feet (122m), has been the scene of scores of fatal climbing accidents and it is sad that so many have died at the same spot, marked by a stone cross that was intended to be a warning to others. It is fixed, horizontally, at the foot of the 300 ft (91m). northern cliffs, and can be reached only by boat. It is inscribed: "Sacred to the memory of Hubert Stone, of Derby, who fell and died here on or about August 30, 1897, aged 14. God grant that we meet again in the Happier Valley." By the time it is seen by people approaching from the top of the Orme the warning is too late – they have fallen over the edge.

While strolling on the Little Orme in September 1873 Lewis Davies, of Tŷ Ucha, found a tin box containing a note saying: "Prince Leopold, son of the Queen, was at this spot August 23rd, '73, on a visit to Llandudno, staying incognito at the Imperial Hotel; was attended by Major-General Patten on this rough ramble hither. His Royal Highness came by sea from Cowes, Isle of Wight; but is resolved not to do so again, having suffered severely from seasickness. His Royal Highness humorously wishes me to add that he would have much liked to plant a tree on this rock in commemoration of the visit, but was restrained from following the example of Her Majesty, his mother, first because it would be very difficult to get a tree up here; secondly, because if a tree were got up, it would be equally difficult to make it grow; third & last such a proceeding, if carried out, would be likely to create a sensation leading, perhaps, to his identification, of which his Highness commanded me to write the above, because knowing the loyalty of the people he (Prince Leopold) thought it would occasion pleasure to some to know that a son of Victoria stood on this spot." It was signed: "Aide-de-camp Patten."

It was the 1884 auction of the Craig-y-don land that led to the growth of Penrhyn Bay as an important residential suburb, in the wake of the quarrying industry that had created the community of Penrhynside, on the eastern shoulder of the Little Orme. The auction map shows the existence of Vicar's Road, now the A546 Llandudno Road but then the property of the Vicar of Llandrillo-yn-rhos and leading to a tollgate at the intersection of Llanrhos Road and Marine Road. The road had been provided at the instigation of the Reverend Venables Williams at a time when the only alternatives were along the beach or via Mochdre, Llangystennin and Glanwydden. The memory of this venture was perpetuated until 1996 in the name of Toll Bar Newsagent (now Bridget's Beauty Salon). The link between the tollgate and Penrhyn Isaf Road was what we now know as St. David's Road, the modern route to the bottom of Penrhyn Hill being a creation of May 1921.

Glan-y-mor Road, Penrhyn Bay, shortly before the demolition of the World War Two machinegun "pillbox" to make way for the 1955 sea-wall.

The 1884 auction also included much of the land on which the older Penrhynside community already existed as a cluster of smallholdings and quarry workers houses, on the opposite side of the hill to the Nant-y-gamar community. During the 1850s the inhabitants acquired two licensed houses, Cross Keys and Penrhyn Arms. In 1872 the children were able to go to school – to the new Church school at Bodafon, funded by Lady Augusta Mostyn. By 1881 they had a shop. The community was blessed with a profusion of places of worship: Moriah (Wesleyan, 1834/1887), Saron (Presbyterian, 1862/1897), Ebeneser (Congregationalist, 1892), St.Sannan's (Church of England, 1892), and Calfaria (Baptist, 1894).

It was on the golf course, founded in 1900 mostly on the Llandudno side of the Afon Ganol, that 34-years-old actor and aviation pioneer Robert Loraine landed his Farman biplane on 10 August 1910, this being the first aircraft to land in Wales, and also an oversea flying record of 63 miles (101km). Using the pseudonym of Jones, so as to confuse his rivals, he had taken off from a Blackpool air show with the intention of hugging the coast to Anglesey, from where he would cross the Irish Sea to Dublin.

"I was on the point of turning back, for my right arm was becoming numbed by the effort necessary to hold the plane on a level course [due to a problem with the elevator control] when a panorama of such loveliness unfurled before me in the long range of Snowdon's mountains," he later recalled.

More or less simultaneously he spotted New Brighton Tower in a clearing through the ground mist, and that enabled him to steer a course for the Great Orme. He flew on, looked at his watch and realised he had been in the air an hour and a half, and his petrol would be running low. "I happened to be over a golf course. The decisive moment had come. I had to descend," he said.

"I was met by a man who ran out over the greens in pyjamas, waving a toothbrush. He took me to the Clubhouse to breakfast while other members went to rope off my machine. In a very short time crowds began to appear; golf was abandoned for the day as the sightseers surged round the plane and settled down in picnic parties," added Jones/Loraine.

The man in his pyjamas was the club's founder, Henry Goldsmith, whose daughter Olive Wilde told the author how she witnessed the aeroplane's arrival with as much wonderment as if it had arrived from outer space. She recalled that the 18-hole 6,064-yard (5545m) course then had a notice board which read: "Rhos & Penrhyn Bay Golf Club. Llandudno's residential golf club." Initially the members had to wear scarlet jackets with green collars, and brass buttons.

Two months earlier, claimed Jones/Loraine with a good dose of artistic licence, the Archdruid of Wales had prophesied a man with wings would come across the mountains, "and lo and behold a Welsh Jones had descended." He signed countless autographs, using the name Jones, his only Welsh link being service in the Boer War with the Montgomeryshire Yeomanry. After refuelling he sat at the controls for two and a half hours before the police could clear a take-off path through the spectators. He came down again in Anglesey and on the next stage ran out of fuel, forcing him to land in the sea off Howth Head, near Dublin, on 11 September. He returned to the stage but during World War One became a lieutenant-colonel in the Royal Flying Corps and was awarded the DSO and MC. He died in 1935.

The Penrhyn Bay in which Robert Loraine landed was then known to the residents of both Llandudno and Colwyn Bay as "the Klondyke." There were Quarry Cottages in Maes Gwyn Road and some newer houses close by, at the eastern end of Penrhyn Isaf Road – one being the favourite holiday haunt of a young clergyman named Hewlett Johnson, who later became known as the Red Dean (of Canterbury, 1931-63) because of his open Marxist sympathies. Another of these houses was the British base of Prince Jafar Mirza of Fars from 1911 when he entered Harrow, until October 1918 when he died while at Llandudno. He was always accompanied by an exotically dressed Persian bodyguard. Penrhyn Isaf Road took its name from the farm that stood east of the intersection with Benarth Road. One of the farm fields, between Benarth Road and the back of what is now Hafod Road West, was known as Cae Clai, meaning "field of clay," and this was the source of material for a brickworks nearer the cliffs, from where a private railway ran to the end of a long wooden pier located about midway between the present Cliff Road and Maes Gwyn Road. There were many houses made of corrugated iron sheeting, the last being Racalia, in Marine Road, lived in until demolished in 1985, when it was still without an electricity or gas supply. The brickworks site was cleared for housing in 1989. The same pier was used for shipping top-quality building sand from the man-made bowl which was grassed and equipped as a children's play area in 1969, when it was named Prince's Green to commemorate the investiture of the Prince of Wales at Caernarfon Castle.

Britain's first conviction for exceeding the 30 mph (48kph) speed limit was obtained in Llandudno Road, Penrhyn Bay. After four years free of any speed restrictions the new law came into operation at midnight on 17 March 1935. A few minutes later Police Constable Idris Evans, wearing civilian clothes and driving an unmarked car, overtook Mr. C. Lomas, of 15 Queen Street, Rhyl, who subsequently pleaded guilty to travelling at 60 mph (96kph) and was fined £2. A week later Llandudno police used a combination of stopwatches and handkerchief signals to trap seventeen RAC Rally competitors over a measured distance of 220 yards (201m) through Penrhyn Bay. Those who passed through the trap in less than fifteen seconds were prosecuted. Within a fortnight Llandudno had scored 27 speeding convictions compared with 40 in the whole of London. The resultant notoriety and warnings to keep away from Llandudno, notably in the *Sunday Times,* had serious consequences for the holiday trade, and it was 35 years before the RAC Rally returned to Llandudno. On 30 November 1976 the police again used Glan-y-mor Road, Penrhyn Bay, as a vascar speed trap for RAC Rally cars arriving at Llandudno for a special stage around the Great Orme.

Children from this new community could attend either Bodafon School or the first Glanwydden School established in 1877 at Ffolt, for the surrounding agricultural community. Now converted into a house known as 6 Ffolt Cottages, the old school can be readily identified, especially from the rear (which would have been the original front). It stands at the end of a narrow cul-de-sac between the disused Ffolt quarry (which provided the stone for the Grand Hotel) and the bramble infested Baptist cemetery.

By 1908 the tiny school housed 148 pupils from Pydew, Glanwydden, Penrhynside and the embryo Penrhyn Bay, and headmaster Thomas Roberts recorded that teaching was greatly hampered by overcrowding and dampness. On 12 February the county medical officer ordered the closure of the school because of an influenza epidemic, and it remained shut for five weeks. A year later the school was struck by an epidemic of coughing and pneumonia, followed by scarlet fever and chickenpox, prompting H.M. Inspector of Schools to report, in July 1909, that it was "urgently necessary that the new school should be built as speedily as possible."

The earliest reference to the present building was in the Ffolt section of the school logbook, in 1907, when Daniel Evans announced his resignation from the board of managers because he had not been consulted over the site. However he was still a very prominent manager on opening day, four years later, and on his death in 1933! A diversion from the cold, dank, crowded and unhealthy misery of life in the old school found its way into the logbook on 25 October 1909, with a serious mid-morning fire at neighbouring Tŷ'n-celyn farm. Next came a deluge and a December entry noting, perhaps with a touch of "I told you so" malice, that the road outside the new school site, in Penrhyn Bay, was dangerous and impassable due to deep flooding (a problem also recorded in 1925, 1940 and 1946, and which recurred in 2001). In February 1910 came dreadful winds (just as they did 80 years later) "making so much noise that one can hardly be heard in the school. Slates are flying about the yard." Epidemics of whooping cough and diphtheria were to be recorded before the new school was ready.

It was on 2 March 1911 that Glanwyddan school moved to its present site, at Penrhyn Bay, but as the façade bears the date 1910 it was decided to avoid confusion by celebrating the 80th anniversary in 1990 – when, as a governor of the school, the author wrote a commemorative leaflet from its very comprehensive log book. The commodious new building offered no immunity from disease and on 17 June 1912 the headmaster arrived to find his school locked, on the orders of the medical officer. An epidemic of mumps had struck down more than half the pupils. Diphtheria and measles were to follow, and deaths among pupils were commonplace in the early days of the school's history. However, the survivors were incredibly tough, for in May 1914 the headmaster logged a school outing that had involved the children in walking to Mochdre & Pabo railway station, from where they took a train to Llandudno Junction. They then walked into Conwy, continued through the Sychnant pass and on, through Dwygyfylchi, to Penmaenmawr station, from where they took a train to Mochdre for the final walk home!

In November 1914 the children were given a half-day holiday to attend the funeral of the Reverend Spinther James, the local Baptist minister of national fame, whose grave can be seen in front of the old school at Ffolt – which was soon to become a hostel for German prisoners-of-war working on nearby farms. There was another half-day holiday in September 1933 for the unveiling by David Lloyd George of the Lewis Carroll memorial on Llandudno's West Shore.

Behind Glanwyddan school is Ysgol y Creuddyn, the Welsh-medium secondary school opened on 1 September 1981, with an initial 218 founder pupils. It has a novel hexagonal plan, built in phases over the subsequent two years, to provide accommodation for each annual intake until completed.

The Afon Ganol has changed its course many times but it still flows across the golf links and is culverted beneath the 3,584 feet (1092m) long sea wall completed in 1956. During its construction, in 1955, the author was summoned to the site by the superintending engineer to see an ancient quay wall that had been excavated beneath where the sea wall now stands. It was of very

Penrhyn Chapel in 1988. The window above the door, round on the outside and rectangular inside, once housed the coloured heraldic glass design below, depicting the Royal Arms of 1405-1603, incorporating the Welsh dragon of the Tudors, including Elizabeth I. The stone crucifix still exists beneath the outer window.

ancient construction and appeared to have been an extension of the ancient wall that can be seen in the garden of the house called Odstone. This was the site of the ancient harbour of Aber Cerrig Gwynion (meaning river mouth of white stones) through which the Afon Ganol used to discharge into the sea. It was usable until 1687, when there was an unsuccessful lawsuit against one of the Pughs of Penrhyn for having effectively closed it to shipping by spanning it with a bridge, to make a roadway. A further barrier against the ravages of the sea was put in place during 1989-90, in the form of massive loose boulders, to protect the 1956 wall, from which much of the foundations had been scoured away.

Attached to the ancient wall preserved at Odstone (which one can see from the roadway), there is a plaque recording the tradition that Prince Madoc of Gloddaeth sailed from here in 1170 with his ships *Corn Gwynant* and *Pedr Sant,* to land at Mobile, Alabama, and thus discover America 322 years before the more celebrated voyage of Christopher Columbus. There is a matching plaque on the shore at Fort Morgan, Alabama, depicting the Red Dragon and inscribed: "In memory of Prince Madoc, a Welsh explorer, who landed on the shores of Mobile Bay in 1170 and left behind, with the Indians, the Welsh language." Many earlier discoverers of America have since entered the field but in 1792 the London Welsh sent John Evans, of Waunfawr, near Caernarfon, off to America on an unsuccessful search for light skinned Welsh-speaking Red Indians.

Lloyd George's Old Age Pensions Act, 1908, had a strange effect in Penrhyn Bay where a well-known litigant called William Horton had bought a lot of land in 1897. He owned the traditional shore road, behind the present sea wall, and along which he had allowed the Llandudno & Colwyn Bay Electric Railway to lay their track in 1907. When Lloyd George was asked how he proposed to finance his pensions of five shillings (25p) a week for the over-seventies (with 7s.6d. – 37½p – for married couples), he replied: "I have no nest eggs. I am looking for someone's hen-roost to rob next year." Horton retaliated by erecting what he called the Budget Gate, between Penrhyn Bay and Rhos-on-Sea, to reimburse himself the extra taxes he anticipated. In 1911 he sold the road to the tram company who continued to collect the toll until they went into voluntary liquidation in 1961, the liquidators continuing to collect it until 1963 when the Llandudno and Colwyn Bay councils bought the road and gave it its first proper surface. One of the more vivid memories of the author's youth is of walking up and down the holidaymakers queuing to pay their toll, advising them of a free and better detour. When the toll house was demolished in 1963 its notice board, listing the charges, still demanded a penny for passage with a perambulator, light handcart or pedal-cycle, although pedestrians and cyclists had been able to avoid paying since 1956 by walking along the sea wall promenade. Cars were charged a shilling (5p), as was a cart drawn by one horse, but a two-horse cart was charged 1s.6d (7½p).

The eastern shoulder of the Little Orme has been absorbed into the Penrhyn Beach estate which was developed in the 1970s, to bring a more balanced age structure into a suburb formerly noted for its unusually high proportion of retired residents. It is a change that has brought in its wake a supermarket opened in 1975 on the site of Tŷ'n Rhewl farm. The working floor of the old quarry, behind the estate, remains a pleasant public open space. Its 1941 gun emplacements for the heavy artillery of the Coast Artillery School were hidden in 1976, some by partial demolition and the two more formidable round forts by being covered with earth. However the latter were uncovered and demolished in February 1986, when the rubble was dumped in the lower level of the old quarry. Perhaps one of these interesting gun emplacements should have been preserved as a piece of local history. The 1851 Coast Artillery School from Shoeburyness was evacuated to the Great Orme in 1940 after the collapse of France, and was extended to Penrhyn Bay the following year. After the guns were fired for practice salvoes a War Department assessor would walk around Penrhyn Bay processing claims for window damage.

From time to time RAF Lysander short take-off and landing aircraft associated with the Artillery

School would land in the fields of Gloddaeth Isaf farm, opposite Glanwydden school. The first use of this land as a temporary airfield was in August 1932, when two former RAF pilots, Randall Stevens and F.W. Horder, offered 5s (25p) flights from here in their Spartan aircraft – attracting about a hundred people a day. They also made one emergency landing on Bodafon Fields. The last aircraft to use the site was a Piper Cherokee, G-AXRL, which lost its front undercarriage and tipped up on its nose when landed by Dr. Dafydd Alun Jones in September 1970. Nine months later he lost a wing when landing in a field near Prestatyn.

From the seafront at Penrhyn Bay one can see an oil rig some 14 miles (22.5km) out to sea, usually with a spectacular flame rising high above it from the burning off of waste fumes. After a decade of exploration it began delivering gas in 1995 to a land depot at the old Point of Ayr colliery site, and feeds a purpose-built electricity generating station at Connah's Quay. It has a projected life of 20 years, and is one of a network of four platforms in Liverpool Bay.

Strangers should beware of the mini roundabout at the cross roads of Llandudno Road, Marine Road and Llanrhos Road. When it was being laid out in 1995, with 29 new road signs, both the Liberal Democrat and Conservative parties claimed credit for it in their election literature. When the accidents began to pile up, including a police car, because of inadequate sight lines, the politicians fell silent – but we are still left with their unnecessary hazard!

Little Orme quarry hoppers, photographed in 1982. Below is seen the last of the Little Orme gun emplacements, photographed in 1970.

In 1920 Llandudno adopted the ruined village of Mametz, and helped pay for its reconstruction, in recognition of the massacre at Mametz Wood of the volunteers recruited at Llandudno, for Lloyd George's Welsh Army. Not surprisingly in a world of political camouflage, one will not find Mametz listed among the official battles, and matching battle honours of World War One, yet it claimed 4,000 men, killed and wounded, of the 38th Welsh Division during only two days in 1916 – victims of corrupt politicians, obsolete generals and German bullets.

With the 53rd Welsh Division of pre-war Territorial Army volunteers on its way to war in the Mediterranean, David Lloyd George, the MP for Llandudno, called for a new 38th Welsh Division of volunteers to serve in France. "We shall march through terror to triumph," he told an audience of London Welshmen, when calling for the raising of a Welsh Army Corps, approved by the Army Council in October 1914. "It is important we should secure the cream of the youth of this country for this Welsh army," he added.

With only 5% of the British population, Wales provided 7% of the Army volunteers, but Lloyd George had to make do with just one division for his intended Army Corps, which he put under the command of his Liberal Party cronies. The 38th Division's twelve new battalions were raised and trained at Llandudno (Royal Welch Fusiliers), Colwyn Bay (Welch Regiment and South Wales Borderers) and Rhyl (Welch Regiment). Ivor Philipps, MP, who had once served as a lieutenant in the Indian Army, was appointed Brigadier-General, and two months later was promoted to Major-General in overall command. Lloyd George's son Gwilym (the future MP) was given the safe job of ADC to the general. David Davies, MP, with no military experience of any kind, was appointed Lieutenant-Colonel commanding the 14th (Carnarvon & Anglesey) Battalion, Royal Welch Fusiliers.

The 1st (North Wales) Brigade [later designated 113 Brigade] was headquartered at Llandudno in December 1914, under Brigadier Owen Thomas. It comprised the 13th (1st North Wales), 14th (Carnarvon & Anglesey), 15th (1st London Welsh), and 16th (2nd North Wales) battalions [and later the 17th Bn] of the Royal Welch Fusiliers. By 2 March 1915 the *Daily Post* was able to report: "Llandudno has today entertained the largest crowd of excursionists that has ever honoured the town with a visit in the winter season. They came, thousands upon thousands of them, men, women and children from all parts of North Wales, not attracted by the sea ... but to take part in the first inspection of the 1st Brigade of the Welsh Army Corps, to lionise the Chancellor of the Exchequer [i.e. Lloyd George], and to celebrate St. David's Day in an entirely new fashion." Lloyd George himself was there to proclaim the march past "One of the most magnificent spectacles I have ever seen."

The Llandudno Brigade was soon on the Somme, eventually to be ordered to take Mametz Wood, which German field engineers had spent two relatively quiet years converting into one of the best defensive positions on the entire front. Undergrowth concealed countless coils of barbed wire and the trees hid a network of fortified machine-gun positions. The only approach was across 400 yards (366m) of open field. Field Marshal Haig did not particularly want Mametz Wood but was responding to France's Marshal Joffre, who reasoned that as the Germans would not surrender it, they would reinforce it in proportion to the number of British lives Haig was prepared to commit to the slaughter, thus relieving the pressure on French troops at Verdun, where there was no real prize to be gained by either side.

Declaring the wood was either deserted or would be quickly abandoned, Haig's headquarters ordered frontal attacks from opposite flanks by the 17th and 38th Divisions. On the eve of the battle Lloyd George withdrew his friend Lieut-Colonel David Davies (a generous contributor to Liberal Party funds) and appointed him Parliamentary Private Secretary in London (later becoming Lord Davies of Llandinam). Major-General Philipps was recalled to London, taking with him his ADC, Lieutenant Gwilym Lloyd George.

On 10 July 1916 Lieutenant-Colonel Ronald James Walter Carden, commanding the 16th (2nd North Wales) RWF, told his men: "Make your peace with God. You are going to take that position, and some of us won't come back." They joined in singing *Jesu, Lover of My Soul,* in impressive Welsh choral tradition, fixed bayonets to their rifles and rushed over the slight ridge and down the slope into the open field. Colonel Carden was dead within a few minutes, having reached the very edge of the wood. Command of David Davies's 14th Battalion, comprising all the volunteers from the Llandudno district, was thrust upon Major Robert Mills, a Boer War veteran of limited military experience who was killed an hour or so after his appointment. In two days of fighting the 38th Welsh Division lost 1,187 men killed and 2,806 wounded, many very seriously.

Thereafter Mametz was an emotive name in Llandudno. When it was realised that the little French village had been totally destroyed by shelling, the people of Llandudno immediately empathised with its returning citizens, and in 1920 adopted Mametz. Returning survivors of the 38th Welsh Division were among those who contributed to the Llandudno fund to help restore the French village 400 miles (644km) away.

Veterans and their descendants had to wait until 11 July 1987, the 71st anniversary of the battle, before a memorial was erected on the ridge down which the Llandudno Brigade had run into the jaws of hidden enemy machine guns. The people of Mametz had long since named the ground Vallée des Gallois, in honour of the Welshmen who had died there. Many of the 250 Welsh people who attended the unveiling shed a tear as the band of the Royal Regiment of Wales led the singing of *Jesu, Lover of My Soul.* The memorial comprises a four-sided column of Welsh granite, surmounted by a steel Red Dragon trampling through barbed wire, made by David Petersen. The badges of the three Welsh infantry regiments of World War One are carved into the sides of the column. The famous Flanders poppy was in full bloom in Picardy and a single flower was placed at the foot of the memorial by the Reverend Evan Sedgmore, with the words: "A symbol of a life given, and of the link between our fallen brethren and those who remain."

After the singing of the national anthems of Wales, France and the United Kingdom the visitors were entertained at the Mairie (Town Hall), where the Mayor asked: "Who are the Llandudno representatives?" Alas, Llandudno Town Council had overlooked the event, and shamefacedly the author and his son, Major Mervyn Wynne Jones, of the Royal Welch Fusiliers, stepped forward to fill the breach. They were shown archival documents relating to the 1920 adoption, including details of Llandudno's donation of 9521 francs towards the 100,000-franc cost of restoring the village's water supply.

As one might expect of the French, there is now a Bois de Mametz wine – actually a Côtes du Rhone – with a coloured label illustrating the 38th Division memorial guarded by two buglers of the Royal Welch Fusiliers, in scarlet tunics. The label also shows their 1916 predecessors battling their way into the woods.

After the disaster at Mametz the dead and wounded were replaced to bring the 38th Division up to full strength for further bloody battles. One of those replacements was Private Ellis Humphrey Evans, of Trawsfynydd, forever famous as the tragic poet Hedd Wyn. He enlisted in February 1917 and during his basic training began writing his poem for that year's National Eisteddfod, on the stipulated title of *Yr Arwr* (The Hero). After basic training he was posted home to help as a khaki-clad ploughman, and during that period he more or less completed his poem. But for those seven twilight weeks of hybrid soldier, ploughman and poet Wales would never have known the poignant drama of Y Gadair Ddu (The Black Chair). He overstayed his agricultural posting by two days, in order to finish his poem, and by way of punishment was immediately posted to Flanders, as one of a reinforcement draft for the 15th Battalion RWF. It was on his way to eternity that he rewrote the final version of his poem which he posted off to the National Eisteddfod under the pseudonym of "Fleur de lis." A bullet through the chest killed him at Pilckem on 31 July 1917, a few days before "Fleur-de-lis" was called out from the Eisteddfod stage, as winner of the bardic chair. There being no response from the pavilion, which was at Birkenhead that year, the officials discovered that the owner of the pseudonym was the dead Private Evans. His chair was draped in black for the remainder of the eisteddfod, and then delivered to his home, Yr Ysgwrn, Trawsfynydd.

Mametz in 1918. The Welsh Division memorial, guarded by buglers of the Royal Welch Fusiliers, is depicted on the label of the modern Bois de Mametz wine.

An early view of the bay showing initial development.

A similar view, with the same properties on the seafront, showing the layout of the promenade and the roof of the Pavilion (left, bottom).

It is interesting to compare this street layout with the last scene: it is clearly earlier. Boats used to take copper ore from Gt Orme's mines from here and some of these boats could have been used for the shipments. The promenade had still to be built.

The obvious difficulty created by the lack of a quay is seen here.

This view shows the new promenade and the kiosk for the pier. There are no cars visible and development does not extend very far inland. Note the Conwy estuary in the distance.

Another view towards West Shore showing the new town clustered close to the bay and no promenade.

A late Victorian view of the pier and its extension down to the Pavilion.

The pier from Gt Orme.

Steamers plied around the coast and over to Liverpool, Bangor, Blackpool, Caernarfon, Holyhead and Douglas on the Isle of Man, stopping off at the Llandudno pier head.

The entrance to the pier after the construction of The Pavilion.

A close up of the Pavilion, now demolished, but the iron columns remain intact.

A view of the Pavilion, The Grand Hotel and the pier.

An early view of The Promenade in pre-motor car days showing the Pavilion and Grand Hotel, with numerous beach carriages on the waterfront.

Another view over the roof of the Pavilion towards North Parade.

Fashions may have changed but walking the prom seems a timeless pastime. Boats moored by the prom are less usual now as is a horse and trap on the sand!

A crowd around a street entertainer, possibly with performing birds, the pier kiosk is beyond.

Bathing machines on the beach. Note the man on the horse; was this the way the huts were moved about? below: Donkeys awaiting riders and customers boarding the boats in the distance.

Carriages on the Promenade. The ladies are in the typical mid-Victorian fashion of black dresses.

The Little Orme about 100 years (or more) ago.

The late Messers Joe Parry and Alf Allan, in the Court Scene, Happy Valley, Llandudno, 1902.

Edwardian crowd at Happy Valley.

The pier from Gt Orme. A steamer is reversing from the pier head. The passengers may be seen streaming down the pier.

The Great Orme Tramway with a tram making the ascent.

Another full tram on the way up Gt Orme.

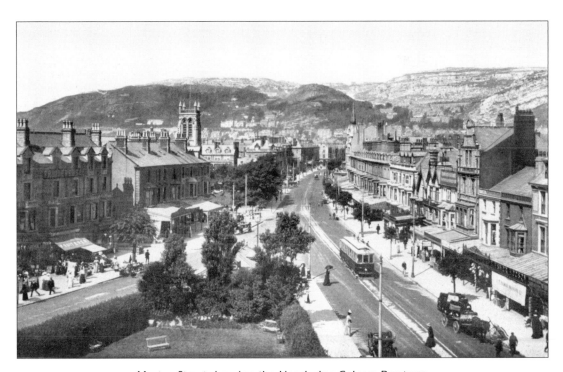

Mostyn Street showing the Llandudno-Colwyn Bay tram.

An early view across the fields towards the hill known as Bryn Euryn.
The hill in the background is the Little Orme.

The former Craigside Hydro from Little Orme.

Gloddaeth Hall in former days; it is now a school. The original part is on the right and saw service in the Civil War, as did the cannon just visible nearto the entrance right of the steps.

Lady Forester's convalescent home, now the North Wales Medical Centre (see p.127).

Launching the original lifeboat in a stormy sea.

The Station Hotel and Conwy Road, Llandudno Junction.

INDEX